Joel, Amos, Obadiah
Turmoil Among the Nations

Joel, Amos, Obadiah
Turmoil Among the Nations

Dr. Bo Wagner

Word of His Mouth Publishers
Mooresboro, NC

All Scripture quotations are taken from the **King James Version** of the Bible.

ISBN: 978-1-941039-59-5
Printed in the United States of America
©2025 Dr. Bo Wagner

Word of His Mouth Publishers
Mooresboro, NC
www.wordofhismouth.com

All rights reserved. No part of this publication may be reproduced in any form without the prior written permission of the publisher, except for quotations in printed reviews.

Table of Contents

Chapter	Page
Intro	7

Joel
1	Tell It to Your Children's Children's Children	11
2	Who Knows?	25
3	The LORD Will Do Great Things	37
4	The Valley Of Decision	51

Amos
5	The Shepherd and The Wolves	69
6	Over The Target	83
7	Jilted	97
8	Prepare To Meet Thy God	111
9	What Are You Looking For?	123
10	Be Careful What You Ask For	137
11	Don't Rest Easy	151
12	When the Preaching Gets Personal	163
13	From The Fruit To The Famine	177
14	The Most Unlikely "Happily Ever After"	189

Obadiah
15	Have You Heard The Rumor About Edom?	207
	Works Cited	221
	Other Books by Dr. Bo Wagner	223

Introduction

The paths of Joel, Amos, and Obadiah may never have crossed. So little is known about them, especially about when they ministered, that their lives may not have even overlapped in time. What we do know about them is that all three were harbingers of doom to the nations, a great many nations. And while Hosea brought a message of love and hope in spite of the coming judgment, these three books are of a decidedly less hopeful nature.

Within these three messages and messengers of judgment, though, there are both glorious truths concerning the nature of God and grand prophecies of the future. So even without the feel-good ending of the biographical and theological portions of Hosea, these three books are equally worth studying.

Joel
Turmoil In Judah

Chapter One
Tell It to Your Children's Children's Children

Joel 1:1 *The word of the LORD that came to Joel the son of Pethuel.* **2** *Hear this, ye old men, and give ear, all ye inhabitants of the land. Hath this been in your days, or even in the days of your fathers?* **3** *Tell ye your children of it, and let your children tell their children, and their children another generation.* **4** *That which the palmerworm hath left hath the locust eaten; and that which the locust hath left hath the cankerworm eaten; and that which the cankerworm hath left hath the caterpiller eaten.* **5** *Awake, ye drunkards, and weep; and howl, all ye drinkers of wine, because of the new wine; for it is cut off from your mouth.* **6** *For a nation is come up upon my land, strong, and without number, whose teeth are the teeth of a lion, and he hath the cheek teeth of a great lion.* **7** *He hath laid my vine waste, and barked my fig tree: he hath made it clean bare, and cast it away; the branches thereof are made white.* **8** *Lament like a virgin girded with sackcloth for the husband of her youth.* **9** *The meat offering and the drink offering is cut off from the house of the LORD; the priests, the LORD'S ministers, mourn.* **10** *The field is wasted, the land mourneth; for the corn is wasted: the new wine is dried up, the oil languisheth.* **11** *Be ye ashamed, O ye husbandmen; howl, O ye vinedressers, for the wheat and* *for the barley; because the harvest of the field is perished.* **12** *The vine is dried up, and the fig tree languisheth; the pomegranate tree, the palm tree also, and the apple tree, even all the trees of the field, are withered: because joy is withered away from the sons of men.* **13** *Gird yourselves, and lament, ye priests: howl, ye ministers of the altar: come, lie all night in sackcloth, ye ministers of my God: for the meat offering and the drink offering is withholden from the house of your God.* **14** *Sanctify ye a fast, call a solemn assembly, gather the elders and all the inhabitants of the land into the house of the LORD your God, and cry unto the LORD,* **15** *Alas for the day! for the day of the LORD is at hand, and as a destruction from the Almighty shall it come.* **16** *Is not the meat cut off before our eyes, yea, joy and gladness from the house of our God?* **17** *The seed is rotten under their clods, the garners are laid desolate, the barns are broken down; for the corn is withered.* **18** *How do the beasts groan! the herds of cattle are perplexed, because they have no pasture; yea, the flocks of sheep are made desolate.* **19** *O LORD, to thee will I cry: for the fire hath devoured the pastures of the wilderness, and the flame hath burned all the trees of the field.* **20** *The beasts of the field cry also unto thee: for the rivers of waters are dried up, and the fire hath devoured the pastures of the wilderness.*

The bare biography of the prophet

Joel 1:1 *The word of the LORD that came to Joel the son of Pethuel.*

With many of the Old Testament prophets, it is comparatively easy to wrap our minds around them as a person due to the sheer amount of information given concerning them.

And then there are prophets like Joel.

With a prophet like Hosea, we are given both a great deal of information about his background and a great deal of information about his life.

With a prophet like Elijah, we are given almost nothing concerning his background, but then we are given a lengthy and picturesque description of his life.

With a prophet like Zephaniah, we know a good bit about his background but next to nothing about his life

But with Joel, we know little to nothing about his background or his life. All we know is his name, Joel, which means Jehovah is God, and the fact that he was the son of a man named Pethuel, of whom we know nothing.

Based on what we read in the book of Joel, he was probably chronologically one of the earliest of the minor prophets, seems to have been a prophet in Judah, and likely prophesied in Jerusalem.

The brutal destruction of the land

Joel 1:2 Hear this, ye old men, and give ear, all ye inhabitants of the land. Hath this been in your days, or even in the days of your fathers? 3 Tell ye your children of it, and let your children tell their children, and their children another generation. 4 That which the palmerworm hath left hath the locust eaten; and that which the locust hath left hath the cankerworm eaten; and that which the cankerworm hath left hath the caterpiller eaten.

Notably absent from the entire book of Joel are the names of kings—or anyone else, for that matter. The only two names of people in the entire book are Joel and his father Pethuel in the very first verse. There are names of places that came from the names of people, things like Judah and Edom, but the only two actual names of people in the entire book are in verse one of chapter one. This book was not written to kings or princes; it was written to absolutely everyone, since everyone was being affected by what was happening.

And Joel wanted to make sure that even those not yet born would never forget:

Joel 1:2 *Hear this, ye old men, and give ear, all ye inhabitants of the land. Hath this been in your days, or even in the days of your fathers?* **3** *Tell ye your children of it, and let your children tell their children, and their children another generation.*

The disaster they were facing was so severe that Joel proclaimed it to be utterly unprecedented, at least for several generations back. And here again was that disaster:

Joel 1:4 *That which the palmerworm hath left hath the locust eaten; and that which the locust hath left hath the cankerworm eaten; and that which the cankerworm hath left hath the caterpiller eaten.*

Many of the prophets, both major and minor, center around invading human armies and coming captivities. Joel centers around something just as dangerous but decidedly less human: insects. Verse four describes four waves of four stages of locusts descending on the land and devouring everything in sight.

Here is how Jamieson, Faussett, and Brown describe this:

> "Four species or stages of locusts, rather than four different insects, are meant. Literally, (1) the gnawing locust; (2) the swarming locust; (3) the licking locust; (4) the consuming locust; forming a climax to the most destructive kind. The last is often three inches long, and the two antennae, each an inch long. The two hinder of its six feet are larger than the rest, adapting it for leaping. The first 'kind' is that of the locust,

having just emerged from the egg in spring, and without wings. The second is when at the end of spring, still in their first skin, the locusts put forth little ones without legs or wings. The third, when after their third casting of the old skin, they get small wings, which enable them to leap the better, but not to fly. Being unable to go away till their wings are matured, they devour all before them, grass, shrubs, and bark of trees: translated 'rough caterpillars' (Jer 51:27). The fourth kind [is] the matured, winged locusts." (Jamieson, 2:511)

Locusts were not at all a surprising thing in those days and in that area of the world. But this particular horde of locusts was so massive and so all-consuming that everyone was at risk of death by starvation. They simply did not leave anything behind that anyone could survive off of; they wiped the face of the earth clean in Joel's land.

It would not take Joel long to point out that this was not just a natural disaster. As was most always the case, this was a divine judgment from God brought about by the sin of the people:

Joel 1:5 *Awake, ye drunkards, and weep; and howl, all ye drinkers of wine, because of the new wine; for it is cut off from your mouth.*

Among other things, many of the people were drunkards. And as is so often the case with such, they were oblivious to the danger bearing down on them. Everyone was at risk of starving to death, but they were sleeping off their latest drunken binge. Joel, though, singled them out as this book begins as people who needed to be awakened immediately. The reason he gave them to wake up was so that they could begin weeping and howling.

You see, it wasn't just the wheat that had been eaten up; all the vineyards had been devoured as well. It takes years to establish a vineyard to the point of fruitfulness. So, these drunks were about to awake to the horrible news that they were going to starve to death and would not have any booze to keep them blissfully and ignorantly happy along the way to their soon-coming graves.

Joel 1:6 *For a nation is come up upon my land, strong, and without number, whose teeth are the teeth of a lion, and he hath the cheek teeth of a great lion.*

The nation Joel refers to in verse six is the locust horde from verse four. This is not a nation of people; it is a nation of munching, flying, devouring insects. And Joel was not speaking in hyperbolic terms when he called them strong without number; they are strong enough to eat everything in sight and can be found in numbers that are nearly unfathomable. Swarms even today typically can occupy one hundred square kilometers which will contain between 4 billion and 8 billion locusts, with the ability to consume the equivalent of what at least 3.5 million people would eat in a day. (Roussi, 2020)

With the way Joel described this devastating swarm of locusts, it is reasonable to assume that they were facing something even much larger than that.

Joel described these locusts this way: *whose teeth are the teeth of a lion, and he hath the cheek teeth of a great lion.* This was a way of describing how deadly their bite was. Mind you, it was produce rather than people they were biting, but death was the result nonetheless.

Joel 1:7 *He hath laid my vine waste, and barked my fig tree: he hath made it clean bare, and cast it away; the branches thereof are made white.*

These locusts were so voracious that they had eaten all the vines and then proceeded to eat every bit of the bark off of the fig trees, taking the trunk and every branch down to the white fleshy pulp beneath it. This would result in the death of those trees and the loss of them as a food source.

Joel 1:8 *Lament like a virgin girded with sackcloth for the husband of her youth.*

In case anyone was not understanding how serious things were, say, perhaps, those drunks who were just being awakened, Joel instructed everyone to weep and cry like a young, espoused lady who was on her way to the marriage altar only to have her espoused husband die before they could say "I do."

For Joel to use a word picture like that, you know that the devastation was beyond the power of human tongue to ever adequately describe. This could very well have ended up with all of Judah simply ceasing to exist.

Joel 1:9 *The meat offering and the drink offering is cut off from the house of the LORD; the priests, the LORD'S ministers, mourn.* **10** *The field is wasted, the land mourneth; for the corn is wasted: the new wine is dried up, the oil languisheth.*

Verse nine is one of the reasons we surmise that Joel was a prophet in the Southern Kingdom of Judah. He speaks here of the house of the Lord, the Temple, the offerings, and the priests.

But when he spoke of those things, it was not a positive mention. Everything in the House of God was suffering because of what the locusts had done. There was simply nothing to offer; the grain for the grain offerings was gone, the oil that would have come from the olive trees was gone, and by extension, we know that the livestock was either dead or dying. The only time the Jews would have been familiar with anything remotely similar was when they were on the other side of the coin from it during the plagues of God against Egypt that led up to the Exodus.

Joel 1:11 *Be ye ashamed, O ye husbandmen; howl, O ye vinedressers, for the wheat and for the barley; because the harvest of the field is perished.* **12** *The vine is dried up, and the* *fig tree languisheth; the pomegranate tree, the palm tree also, and the apple tree, even all the trees of the field, are withered: because joy is withered away from the sons of men.*

Husbandmen and vinedressers were both descriptions of people who grew produce for a living. Husbandmen would be similar to our word for farmer, and vinedressers were those who grew things that grow on vines, most notably grapes. God told both of those people to be ashamed and howl at what had taken place. And this once again gives us a hint as to the moral nature of this calamity. If this were merely a matter of these people doing their very best and yet conditions being against them to such a degree that they failed in their quest to grow crops, howling may be a bit warranted, but shame certainly would not. No, this was a matter of people who should have been successful in growing the things that would keep people alive but failed because their departure from a right walk with God had led to His judgment in the form of locusts. And look again at some of the specifics of the devastation:

Joel 1:11 *Be ye ashamed, O ye husbandmen; howl, O ye vinedressers, for the **wheat** and for the **barley**; because the harvest of the field is perished.* **12** *The **vine** is dried up, and the **fig** tree languisheth; the **pomegranate** tree, the **palm tree** also, and the **apple** tree, even **all the trees of the field**, are withered:*

Wheat, barley, grapes, figs, pomegranates, dates from the date palm, apples, all of that and much more were simply gone.

Now let's look at verses eleven and twelve together one more time, focusing on the very last phrase of verse twelve, because the way it is worded can be a bit confusing if you are not paying attention:

Joel 1:11 *Be ye ashamed, O ye husbandmen; howl, O ye vinedressers, for the wheat and for the barley; because the harvest of the field is perished.* **12** *The vine is dried up, and the fig tree languisheth; the pomegranate tree, the palm tree also,* *and the apple tree, even all the trees of the field, are withered: <u>because joy is withered away from the sons of men.</u>*

Let me tell you what this phrase is not saying. It is not saying that the vine is dried up and the fig tree languishing and everything else dying because (as a result of) the fact that joy is withered away from the sons of men. It was not unhappy people who had eaten up all the crops; it was locusts that did that. This goes back to the first phrase in verse eleven, and it is the second thing that God expects them to do based on what is happening. Let's read them again, and I will put in some explanatory words to help you see how it goes:

Joel 1:11 *Be ye ashamed, O ye husbandmen; howl, O ye vinedressers,* [first of all] *for the wheat and for the barley; because the harvest of the field is perished.* **12** *The vine is dried up, and the fig tree languisheth; the pomegranate tree, the palm tree also, and the apple tree, even all the trees of the field, are withered:* [and secondly] *because* [as a result,] *joy is withered away from the sons of men.*

No food, no joy, because everyone is either dead or dying.

Joel 1:13 *Gird yourselves, and lament, ye priests: howl, ye ministers of the altar: come, lie all night in sackcloth, ye ministers of my God: for the meat offering and the drink offering is withholden from the house of your God.*

Verse thirteen is Joel speaking to the clergy of the land. He told them to gird themselves, meaning to put on what they should be wearing, which in this case he specifies as sackcloth. He told them to lament and to howl; those who normally had the clean and respectable job of ministering about the altar were now to lay aside all of that respectability and bare the emotions of their heart, weeping and wailing before the LORD on behalf of the people. And they were to do so with the realization that what was going on in the land was not just affecting people and households but the very House of God itself. No meat offerings were able to be given; no drink offerings were able to be given; the service of the LORD could not take place. All of the nation revolved around what took place in the Temple, and all of that had ground to a halt in light of the disaster that had just befallen.

The bitter cry to the LORD

Joel 1:14 *Sanctify ye a fast, call a solemn assembly, gather the elders and all the inhabitants of the land into the house of the LORD your God, and cry unto the LORD,*

Facing the unparalleled disaster that threatened to destroy them all, Joel, the prophet of God, prescribed the course of action we see in verse fourteen. The people were to sanctify a fast, meaning to set aside a time period in which everyone would abstain from any food that they still had, and they were to call for a solemn assembly. Both the elders and the inhabitants of the land, those who were in charge and those who were merely citizens, were to come together into the House of God and cry out to the LORD.

All of this gives us both some information about the time period and a prescription for how to handle any disaster, regardless of the time period. The fact that everyone was to come to the Temple lets us know that the Temple was still standing and still very much in use; so, this was early in the history of the southern kingdom, not late. The fact that everyone was to come together in God's house to cry out to the LORD is a reminder that that should still be our prescribed course of action in any time of trouble.

The House of God should not merely be a place we come once or twice a week to sing the same songs we have always sung and hear the same messages we have always heard; it should be a place we are called to on any and every day of the week when there is a need so great that we as a people need God's immediate attention.

Joel 1:15 *Alas for the day! for the day of the LORD is at hand, and as a destruction from the Almighty shall it come.*

The word *alas* is an extremely rare word in Scripture, occurring only sixteen times. And in case you want to know how much a harbinger of disaster it is, six of those sixteen times are found in the book of the Revelation. Here in Joel 1:15, it is from the word *ahaw*, and it means something like *Oh no!* in our vernacular.

So what was Joel "oh noing" about? Not just the swarm of locusts; he saw more to it than that. Here it is again, *Alas for the day! <u>for the day of the LORD is at hand, and as a destruction from the Almighty shall it come</u>.*

When you see words as significant as <u>the day of the LORD is at hand</u>, you should definitely slow down and take note—and we shall do so now.

We should begin by noting how significant this is in the tiny book of Joel. Here is what we find in only three chapters:

Joel 1:15 *Alas for the day! for <u>the day of the LORD</u> is at hand, and as a destruction from the Almighty shall it come.*

Joel 2:1 *Blow ye the trumpet in Zion, and sound an alarm in my holy mountain: let all the inhabitants of the land tremble: for <u>the day of the LORD</u> cometh, for it is nigh at hand;*

Joel 2:11 *And the LORD shall utter his voice before his army: for his camp is very great: for he is strong that executeth his word: for <u>the day of the LORD</u> is great and very terrible; and who can abide it?*

Joel 2:31 *The sun shall be turned into darkness, and the moon into blood, before the great and the terrible <u>day of the LORD</u> come.*

Joel 3:14 *Multitudes, multitudes in the valley of decision: for <u>the day of the LORD</u> is near in the valley of decision.*

Out of the twenty-five times *the day of the LORD* is mentioned in Scripture, Joel, just three chapters long, has five of those references. Twenty percent of the references to the day of the Lord in Scripture are found right here in the tiny book of Joel; this is the central theme and thought of his writing.

By the use of the LORD in all caps, we know that by title, he is referring to this as the day of Jehovah God. As to what that means, Charles Feinberg gave an excellent explanation of its usage:

> "After the rapture 'the day of Jehovah' begins. It comprises the time of the Great Tribulation on earth, the seventieth week of Daniel 9:27, and the time of the rule of the Messiah of Israel over them in Jerusalem on the throne of David. (See not only the Scriptures noted above in Joel, but Amos 5:18; Zephaniah 1:14-2:2 together with Isaiah 2:1-21 among many scriptures throughout the prophetic books.)" (Feinberg, 74)

Joel, then, in seeing the utter devastation these locusts brought to the land, was prophetically looking ahead in time to the similar yet even greater devastation that will be brought onto the earth during the Great Tribulation. That gives you some sense of how bad the Tribulation will be and how bad the plague of locusts was in Joel's day. The Tribulation Period, more than any other point in human history, will definitely be an "alas, oh no!" kind of thing!

Let us look at verse fifteen one more time before moving on; there is one more thing of which we should take note.

Joel 1:15 *Alas for the day! for the day of the LORD is at hand, and as a destruction from the Almighty shall it come.*

Notice that this will come as a destruction from the Almighty. Both the locusts of Joel's day and the unfathomable devastation of the earth during the seven-year Tribulation Period were/will be supernatural, not natural. There will be no way to pawn off the miraculous occurrences of the Tribulation Period as climate change, corporate greed, or nature doing what nature does. God will make Himself known through judgment to a world that refused to know Him through grace.

Joel 1:16 *Is not the meat cut off before our eyes, yea, joy and gladness from the house of our God?* **17** *The seed is rotten under their clods, the garners are laid desolate, the barns are broken down; for the corn is withered.*

Joel is, in these verses, reiterating what has already been said: the food supply had been cut off, and there was no rejoicing in the House of God because there was neither worship nor anything for the worshippers to bring if they did come. The seed that should have grown had rotted and was decaying under the clods of dirt rather than springing forth into life. The gardens that should have been full of produce were instead desolate. The barns that should have been maintained in order to handle all of the produce were instead broken down and left in disrepair because the corn had withered and died, and there was, therefore, no need for a place in which to store it.

Joel 1:18 *How do the beasts groan! the herds of cattle are perplexed, because they have no pasture; yea, the flocks of sheep are made desolate.*

When man's disobedience has brought the judgment of God on the land, even the animals will suffer for it. As Joel was writing his prophecy for the people, he could hear the beasts of the land groaning in starvation. He could look out of his window or out into the field as he passed by and see herds of cattle utterly confused because they had no pastureland in which to graze, merely dry and cracked parcels of earth that produced nothing for them. He could see what had once been thriving flocks of sheep made utterly desolate, down to their last few members of the flock: malnourished, starving lambs that would not live for much longer.

Joel 1:19 *O LORD, to thee will I cry: for the fire hath devoured the pastures of the wilderness, and the flame hath burned all the trees of the field.*

Joel, of all people, would have been very familiar with our modern sentiment, "When it rains, it pours." Only in his case, they could have used the rain, because not only had they suffered the devastation of the locusts, but fire had then somehow been kindled, burning any scraps and remnants of their pastures and all of the trees of the field.

Joel 1:20 *The beasts of the field cry also unto thee: for the rivers of waters are dried up, and the fire hath devoured the pastures of the wilderness.*

Locusts. Fire. And now drought. The rivers were drying up, resulting in more fires and more rapid spread of the fires, devouring the pastures of the wilderness in addition to their cultivated fields. No wonder Joel said *The beasts of the field cry also unto thee!* In their mournful lowing, the very beasts of the field were calling out to their Creator for help in a time when there seemed none to be had.

Now you know why Joel said, *Tell It To Your Children's Children's Children.* And the most heartbreaking part of it all was that if they had forever and only and always followed God, they could have been telling their children's children's children about God's blessings instead

Chapter Two
Who Knows?

Joel 2:1 *Blow ye the trumpet in Zion, and sound an alarm in my holy mountain: let all the inhabitants of the land tremble: for the day of the LORD cometh, for it is nigh at hand;* **2** *A day of darkness and of gloominess, a day of clouds and of thick darkness, as the morning spread upon the mountains: a great people and a strong; there hath not been ever the like, neither shall be any more after it, even to the years of many generations.* **3** *A fire devoureth before them; and behind them a flame burneth: the land is as the garden of Eden before them, and behind them a desolate wilderness; yea, and nothing shall escape them.* **4** *The appearance of them is as the appearance of horses; and as horsemen, so shall they run.* **5** *Like the noise of chariots on the tops of mountains shall they leap, like the noise of a flame of fire that devoureth the stubble, as a strong people set in battle array.* **6** *Before their face the people shall be much pained: all faces shall gather blackness.* **7** *They shall run like mighty men; they shall climb the wall like men of war; and they shall march every one on his ways, and they shall not break their ranks:* **8** *Neither shall one thrust another; they shall walk every one in his path: and when they fall upon the sword, they shall not be wounded.* **9** *They shall run to and fro in the city; they shall run upon the wall, they shall climb up upon the houses; they shall enter in at the windows like a thief.* **10** *The earth shall* *quake before them; the heavens shall tremble: the sun and the moon shall be dark, and the stars shall withdraw their shining:* **11** *And the LORD shall utter his voice before his army: for his camp is very great: for he is strong that executeth his word: for the day of the LORD is great and very terrible; and who can abide it?* **12** *Therefore also now, saith the LORD, turn ye even to me with all your heart, and with fasting, and with weeping, and with mourning:* **13** *And rend your heart, and not your garments, and turn unto the LORD your God: for he is gracious and merciful, slow to anger, and of great kindness, and repenteth him of the evil.* **14** *Who knoweth if he will return and repent, and leave a blessing behind him; even a meat offering and a drink offering unto the LORD your God?*

In chapter one, we were given the reason for the writing of the book of Joel: a locust swarm of supernatural proportions had descended upon the land, eating everything in sight and threatening to starve the population into extinction. Additionally, drought and wildfires were taking their toll at the exact same time.

Joel used all of this to point to an even greater future judgment, the day of the LORD.

And he opens chapter two by continuing to look to that future judgment in light of their present calamity.

A warning

Joel 2:1 *Blow ye the trumpet in Zion, and sound an alarm in my holy mountain: let all the inhabitants of the land tremble: for the day of the LORD cometh, for it is nigh at hand;*

When we, in our day, think of the trumpet, the image of lovely instruments in the band, things that look like they are made of silver or gold, may come to mind. But that is not at all the kind of trumpet being spoken of here. They did have trumpets similar to that, but those were normally for festive occasions.

This was not a festive occasion. This was not a concert. And this shofar, this ram's horn trumpet that was to be blown, was specifically to be blown as an alarm. It was to signal to the people that disaster in the form of some enemy was upon them.

The location is likewise significant. This alarm was not being sounded in some village on the outskirts of the land; it was to be sounded right there on God's holy mountain in Jerusalem. The devastation was affecting the capital city as much or more than any other part of the land. Because of this, Joel said, *let all the inhabitants of the land tremble.*

If God was willing to let enemies even onto His holy mount, no one in the rest of the land could expect to be spared at all. And once again, though the immediate problem was the locusts of Joel's day, they pointed ahead to a much larger problem. Here again is how Joel ended verse one:

...for the day of the LORD cometh, for it is nigh at hand;

From our perspective, we may look at that warning about the nearness of the day of the Lord and take issue with it. After all, Joel wrote those words approximately 2,700 years ago. But anyone who used to be young and now is old understands one thing very plainly: time passes by incredibly quickly. To you who are older, the days of your youth seem like yesterday.

To the eternal God who authored these words, the day of the LORD was and is indeed near at hand. And for Joel and his people, that plague of locusts was the day of the LORD then and there to them since this was His judgment for sin.

Joel 2:2 *A day of darkness and of gloominess, a day of clouds and of thick darkness, as the morning spread upon the mountains: a great people and a strong; there hath not been ever the like, neither shall be any more after it, even to the years of many generations.*

As in most of this chapter, there is a dual reference to the words of Joel in this verse. This obviously still points ahead in time to the judgment of the Tribulation Period, some details of which we will see very specifically in just a few verses. But it also pointed to what was happening in Joel's day. These locusts were flying and swarming in such numbers that the day itself was dark and gloomy as if smothered by a blanket of thick clouds and darkness. And all of this took place with the rapidity of the morning sun spreading out across the mountains. Only in this case, it was not a cheery sunrise but a consuming locust rise.

In the last chapter, these locusts were referred to as a nation. Here, they are referred to in similar terms: *a great people and a strong; there hath not been ever the like, neither shall be any more after it, even to the years of many generations.*

Joel understood that the supernatural swarm of locusts was so far out of the bounds of the natural that it had never been that way before; for a very long time, it would never be that way again. And so, faced with such a disaster, the warning was given to blow the trumpet and sound the alarm, for all the good it was likely to do.

A wasting

Joel 2:3 *A fire devoureth before them; and behind them a flame burneth: the land is as the garden of Eden before them, and behind them a desolate wilderness; yea, and nothing shall escape them.*

In chapter one, we saw actual fires as part of the judgment upon the land. In this particular case, this fire is a metaphor for the destruction brought on by the locusts; the first half of the verse is explained by the second half of the verse. Just like a raging fire turns a beautiful landscape into a hellscape, these locusts were descending on a land that had been as fruitful as the Garden of Eden out in front of them, and in their wake, they left nothing but a desolate wilderness.

A wailing

At this point in the text, Joel's eye moves from the present to the prophetic. You will understand this quite clearly when you see where else in the Bible these words of Joel are mentioned.

Joel 2:4 *The appearance of them is as the appearance of horses; and as horsemen, so shall they run.*

Joel has been talking about locusts. But suddenly, he gives a rather shocking description of the locusts. He says that they have the appearance of horses and run like the horsemen upon them. So, is there anywhere else in the Bible that we find locusts that look like horses? Yes, there is:

Revelation 9:1 *And the fifth angel sounded, and I saw a star fall from heaven unto the earth: and to him was given the key of the bottomless pit.* **2** *And he opened the bottomless pit; and there arose a smoke out of the pit, as the smoke of a great furnace; and the sun and the air were darkened by reason of the smoke of the pit.* **3** *And there came out of the smoke locusts upon the earth: and unto them was given power, as the scorpions of the earth have power.* **4** *And it was commanded them that they should not hurt the grass of the earth, neither any green thing, neither any tree; but only those men which have not the seal of God in their foreheads.* **5** *And to them it was given that they should not kill them, but that they should be tormented five months: and their torment was as the torment of a scorpion, when he striketh a man.* **6** *And in those days shall men seek death, and shall not find it; and shall desire to die, and death shall flee from them.* **7** *And the shapes of the locusts were like unto horses prepared unto battle; and on their heads were as it were crowns like gold, and their faces were as the faces of men.*

This is the day of the LORD. As Joel was looking at the very natural locusts of his day, though in supernatural numbers, God let his eyes cross the millennia and see into a day still yet future to us, a day when demonic locusts from the bottomless pit will ascend onto the earth as a judgment from God. These locusts that look like horses will have the power of a scorpion's sting in their tail, and they will torment men for five solid months. Men will wish to die, but death will flee from them.

This is what Joel was now beginning to discuss.

Joel 2:5 *Like <u>the noise of chariots</u> on the tops of mountains shall they leap, like the noise of a flame of fire that devoureth the stubble, as a strong people set in battle array.*

Do we read of anything like this in the day of the LORD? Yes:

Revelation 9:9 *And they had breastplates, as it were breastplates of iron; and the sound of their wings was as <u>the sound of chariots</u> of many horses running to battle.*

These creatures will be terrifyingly noisy. People will hear them coming but will not be able to escape.

Joel 2:6 *Before their face the people shall be much pained: all faces shall gather blackness.*

Does this description fit, the description of agony being on everyone's faces? Yes again:

Revelation 9:5 *And to them it was given that they should not kill them, but that they should be **tormented** five months: and their **torment** was as the **torment** of a scorpion, when he striketh a man.*

Torment. Torment. Torment. Scorpion. There is going to be agony etched on everyone's face, and no one will be able to stop it. People's faces will turn black through the pain; this is an indication that the strain and screaming has caused blood vessels to burst, making everyone's faces look like they have been beaten black and blue.

Joel 2:7 *They shall run like mighty men; they shall climb the wall like men of war; and they shall march every one on his ways, and they shall not break their ranks:*

These locusts will be systematic and disciplined. They will go out in ranks and not break those ranks. How will this be possible for "dumb insects?" Here is how:

Revelation 9:11 *And they had a king over them, which is the angel of the bottomless pit, whose name in the Hebrew tongue is Abaddon, but in the Greek tongue hath his name Apollyon.*

This gets even more interesting when you look at another mention of locusts in the Bible:

Proverbs 30:27 *The locusts have no king, yet go they forth all of them by bands;*

Some bugs have a monarch, a queen, usually. But not the locusts. They have no king. But even without a king, they go out in orderly arrangements. Think, then, of how systematically they will be able to move in the pursuit of men when they do have a king. And not just any king; this king is a fallen angel whose Hebrew name is Abaddon and whose Greek name is Apollyon. Both of those names mean "the Destroyer."

This is an angel near in power to Satan himself and just as hateful. He will, in a satanic fury, direct and drive on these demonic locusts, not giving them as much as a second to rest. They are only going to live for a short five months, and Apollyon will make sure that they spend every moment of those five months doing their destructive job.

Naturally, men will try to destroy them. After all, we humans have been in the pest control business for a very long time! Unfortunately for mankind, though, these bugs cannot self-destruct nor be destroyed:

Joel 2:8 *Neither shall one thrust another; they shall walk every one in his path: and when they fall upon the sword, they shall not be wounded.*

They cannot even be wounded, much less destroyed! And they are going to be very diligent in their task:

Joel 2:9 *They shall run to and fro in the city; they shall run upon the wall, they shall climb up upon the houses; they shall enter in at the windows like a thief.*

This is not natural; it is supernatural. These locusts will not content themselves to the field; they will invade each and every house. They will be the monsters under the bed, the terror in the mirror, and the devil in the darkness.

Joel 2:10 *The earth shall quake before them; the heavens shall tremble: the sun and the moon shall be dark, and the stars shall withdraw their shining:*

There will be so many of these locusts that the earth and atmosphere will shake because of them. And they will also blot out the light of the sun, moon, and stars:

Revelation 9:2 *And he opened the bottomless pit; and there arose a smoke out of the pit, as the smoke of a great furnace; and the sun and the air were darkened by reason of the smoke of the pit.*

All of that, this description of these demonic locusts with the demonic king, brings us to a truly jaw-dropping and perhaps unexpected mention in this account:

Joel 2:11 *And the LORD shall utter his voice before <u>his army</u>: for <u>his camp</u> is very great: for he is strong that executeth his word: for the day of the LORD is great and very terrible; and who can abide it?*

Are these locusts demonic? Yes. Do they have a demonic king? Yes again. But the LORD is the owner of the entire horde. They will do what they do at *His* permission. This will be His judgment on a world that has, in so many words, said, "Bring it on, God."

And He will.

A wondering

As verse eleven ends, Joel has now come back from the prophetic to the present. As verse twelve begins, he is going to give a present-day message to his people undergoing this judgment of the locusts:

Joel 2:12 *Therefore also now, saith the LORD, turn ye even to me with all your heart, and with fasting, and with weeping, and with mourning:* **13** *And rend your heart, and not your garments, and turn unto the LORD your God: for he is gracious and merciful, slow to anger, and of great kindness, and repenteth him of the evil.*

Here is what you need to understand as we begin to consider verses twelve and thirteen and then verse fourteen after them: verses twelve and thirteen are Joel relaying the message of the LORD word for word to the people.

And that word was in three parts, as follows.

One, they were to turn to the LORD with all their heart, and with fasting, and with weeping, and with mourning. So, they were to be one hundred percent committed to repentance from sin and following God, they were to show that seriousness by fasting, they were to weep, and they were to mourn.

Their sin and the judgment it brought on the land deserved no less.

Two, they were to rend [tear] their hearts rather than their clothes and turn to the LORD their God. Throughout their history, they were far too often guilty of tearing their clothes in a pretended show of sorrow and repentance when that was all that it was: a show. God expected them to have broken hearts rather than ripped shirts, a repentance proven by an actual turning back to the LORD.

Three, this God they were to turn back to was gracious and merciful, slow to anger, and of great kindness, and One who would repent (turn away from) of the evil, meaning the damage He intended to do to them.

All of that was the words of God that Joel relayed word for word to the people.

And that is what makes verse fourteen so jaw-dropping. Verse fourteen is Joel's words to the people after he had given God's words to the people:

Joel 2:14 *Who knoweth if he will return and repent, and leave a blessing behind him; even a meat offering and a drink offering unto the LORD your God?*

Do you understand what Joel was saying? If we put it in conversation form between him and the people, it would go something like this:

Joel: "God expects us to repent and return to Him with all of our hearts. And He is a merciful and good and gracious God."

Voice from the crowd: "If we do repent and return to Him with all of our hearts, since He is so merciful and good and gracious, will He withdraw this judgment and save us?"

Joel: "Who knows? Maybe if we will return and repent, He will return and repent and leave a blessing behind Him. Maybe He will let there be enough left in the field for even a meat offering and a drink offering unto the LORD your God, so we can worship in His house again with a bit of joy. Maybe. Who knows?"

May I make an excellent suggestion? Never go off into sin to begin with. But if you ever do, be sure and come back before it gets to the point of "Will God still help us? Who knows..."

Chapter Three
The LORD Will Do Great Things

Joel 2:15 *Blow the trumpet in Zion, sanctify a fast, call a solemn assembly:* **16** *Gather the people, sanctify the congregation, assemble the elders, gather the children, and those that suck the breasts: let the bridegroom go forth of his chamber, and the bride out of her closet.* **17** *Let the priests, the ministers of the LORD, weep between the porch and the altar, and let them say, Spare thy people, O LORD, and give not thine heritage to reproach, that the heathen should rule over them: wherefore should they say among the people, Where is their God?* **18** *Then will the LORD be jealous for his land, and pity his people.* **19** *Yea, the LORD will answer and say unto his people, Behold, I will send you corn, and wine, and oil, and ye shall be satisfied therewith: and I will no more make you a reproach among the heathen:* **20** *But I will remove far off from you the northern army, and will drive him into a land barren and desolate, with his face toward the east sea, and his hinder part toward the utmost sea, and his stink shall come up, and his ill savour shall come up, because he hath done great things.* **21** *Fear not, O land; be glad and rejoice: for the LORD will do great things.* **22** *Be not afraid, ye beasts of the field: for the pastures of the wilderness do spring, for the tree beareth her fruit, the fig tree and the vine do yield their strength.* **23** *Be glad then, ye children of Zion, and rejoice in the LORD your God: for* *he hath given you the former rain moderately, and he will cause to come down for you the rain, the former rain, and the latter rain in the first month.* **24** *And the floors shall be full of wheat, and the fats shall overflow with wine and oil.* **25** *And I will restore to you the years that the locust hath eaten, the cankerworm, and the caterpiller, and the palmerworm, my great army which I sent among you.* **26** *And ye shall eat in plenty, and be satisfied, and praise the name of the LORD your God, that hath dealt wondrously with you: and my people shall never be ashamed.* **27** *And ye shall know that I am in the midst of Israel, and that I am the LORD your God, and none else: and my people shall never be ashamed.* **28** *And it shall come to pass afterward, that I will pour out my spirit upon all flesh; and your sons and your daughters shall prophesy, your old men shall dream dreams, your young men shall see visions:* **29** *And also upon the servants and upon the handmaids in those days will I pour out my spirit.* **30** *And I will shew wonders in the heavens and in the earth, blood, and fire, and pillars of smoke.* **31** *The sun shall be turned into darkness, and the moon into blood, before the great and the terrible day of the LORD come.* **32** *And it shall come to pass, that whosoever shall call on the name of the LORD shall be delivered: for in mount Zion and in Jerusalem shall be deliverance, as the LORD hath said, and in the remnant whom the LORD shall call.*

    Locusts had descended upon the land and devoured everything in sight. And this was such an out-of-the-ordinary-sized plague of locusts that Joel knew it was a supernatural occurrence rather than a natural occurrence. The people were under the judgment of God for their behavior.

    Joel used all of this to point ahead in time to the day of the LORD, primarily speaking of the Tribulation Period and the even more devastating judgment it would bring.

And then he said something shocking in chapter two. It went something along the lines of, "Everybody needs to repent. And if you do, maybe, just *maybe*, God will be merciful."

In the last half of chapter two, Joel was going to find out that it was more than a maybe.

An assembly gathering

Joel 2:15 *Blow the trumpet in Zion, sanctify a fast, call a solemn assembly:*

This is now the third time in the book of Joel that we find these words of instruction. Here is where we previously saw them:

Joel 1:14 *Sanctify ye a fast, call a solemn assembly, gather the elders and all the inhabitants of the land into the house of the LORD your God, and cry unto the LORD,*

Joel 2:1 *Blow ye the trumpet in Zion, and sound an alarm in my holy mountain: let all the inhabitants of the land tremble: for the day of the LORD cometh, for it is nigh at hand;*

Once again, the people were to sanctify a fast, meaning to set aside a time period in which everyone would abstain from any food that they still had, and they were to call for a solemn assembly. This was not to be a time of joyful worship; everyone was to come together into the House of God and cry out to the LORD.

Are there times for joyful worship? Certainly. I contend that most of our time together in the House of God should be joyful worship. But when something is going wrong, especially when the land is under the judgment of God because of its sin and everyone is being affected, that is the time to weep and to cry, not to laugh and to celebrate.

Joel 2:16 *Gather the people, sanctify the congregation, assemble the elders, gather the children, and those that suck the* *breasts: let the bridegroom go forth of his chamber, and the bride out of her closet.*

This verse tells us how serious the issue was and how widespread the gathering for repentance was to be. Joel began by saying *Gather the people*, which is a fairly general statement. He follows that with a second general statement, *sanctify the congregation*. So, people and congregation.

But when we use general terms like that, inevitably, someone is going to have themselves excused, just like in every church service.

"I would come, but I…" fill in the blank with whatever excuse comes next.

It seems as though Joel understood that, because he then moves from those two general statements to start covering some very specific categories.

Here are the people he commanded to be there:

…assemble the <u>elders</u>, gather the <u>children</u>, and <u>those that suck the breasts</u>: let <u>the bridegroom</u> go forth of his chamber, and <u>the bride</u> out of her closet.

The elders, the very aged people, were to be there. The children were to be there. Nursing babies were to be there. The husband, preparing to enjoy the first night of his honeymoon, was to be there. The bride preparing to present herself to that husband for their first night together was to be there. This judgment was affecting absolutely everyone; everyone was at risk of dying in short order, so everyone was to drop everything and get to the House of God to weep before the LORD.

Joel 2:17 *Let the priests, the ministers of the LORD, weep between the porch and the altar, and let them say, Spare thy people, O LORD, and give not thine heritage to reproach, that the heathen should rule over them: wherefore should they say among the people, Where is their God?*

A location is given to us in this verse, and it helps to paint the picture of everything that was to be taking place. With all the congregation gathered to Solomon's Temple, the priests, the ministers of the LORD, were to position themselves between the altar of the burnt offering and the porch of the Temple. In between those two points was an open space of about thirty feet. And since it was outside in the courtyard, all the assembled congregation could see what was happening.

Normally, if the priests were in that place, they were at the altar of the burnt offering making a sacrifice to the LORD. But in this case, they had nothing to sacrifice; the devastation in the land had rendered them empty-handed before the LORD.

So instead of a sacrifice of treasure, there was to be a sacrifice of tears.

You can readily imagine the deep impact it made on the people when they saw their priests, men who always operated with confidence in that place as they made their sacrifices, instead weeping helplessly and empty-handed before the Lord.

But the people were not just to see them weep; they were also to hear them speak to the LORD. And Joel told them what they needed to say:

Joel 2:17 *...Spare thy people, O LORD, and give not thine heritage to reproach, that the heathen should rule over them: wherefore should they say among the people, Where is their God?*

There was nothing of the worthiness of the people mentioned in these words, because the people had no worthiness to mention. Instead, there was a plea for mercy, a cry for God to spare His people. Jehovah was to be called to by name and asked to not give His heritage to reproach.

And that is exactly what Israel was, the heritage of the LORD. They are referred to as such in Psalm 94:5, among other places.

The priests were to ask God not to let the heathen rule over them and to not allow the heathens in glee to ask *Where is their God?*

An assurance from the LORD

Joel 2:18 *Then will the LORD be jealous for his land, and pity his people.*

Joel has now moved from the *who knoweth?* of verse fourteen to a very confident *Then will the LORD* here in verse eighteen. God has given him assurance to relate to the people. And the assurance begins with the fact that if all the people will gather to wait before the LORD, and if the priests will intercede as instructed, the LORD will most assuredly be jealous for His land and show pity to His people.

The details of the promise continue in verse nineteen:

Joel 2:19 *Yea, the LORD will answer and say unto his people, Behold, I will send you corn, and wine, and oil, and ye shall be satisfied therewith: and I will no more make you a reproach among the heathen:*

God is so very exact in everything. Look back to what had been taken from them in the first chapter:

Joel 1:10 *The field is wasted, the land mourneth; for the **corn** is wasted: the new **wine** is dried up, the **oil** languisheth.*

Corn. Wine. Oil. All had been devastated by the plague of locusts. So here in Joel 2:19, God mentions those exact three things and the fact that He will restore them all.

The loss of those things had made them a reproach, a laughingstock among the heathen; the restoration of all of those things would stop the mouths of the mockers and reestablish the fact of Israel's relationship with God before everyone's eyes.

How was all of this going to happen? Here is the first part of that answer:

Joel 2:20 *But I will remove far off from you the northern army, and will drive him into a land barren and desolate, with his face toward the east sea, and his hinder part toward the utmost sea, and his stink shall come up, and his ill savour shall come up, because he hath done great things.*

Please keep in mind that the army spoken of here was, once again, an army of insects, not of people. And this verse tells us the direction they came from, the north.

Adam Clarke pointed out that "Syria, which was northward of Judea, was infested with them; and it must have been a northern wind that brought them into Judea, in the time of Joel." (Clarke, 4:663)

God said of this insect army of the North that He would *drive him into a land barren and desolate, with his face toward the east sea, and his hinder part toward the utmost sea, and his stink shall come up, and his ill savour shall come up, because he hath done great things.*

The same God that blew them into the land was going to turn right around and blow them out of the land, with the front columns being blown toward the Dead Sea east of Jerusalem and the back columns extending all the way to the utmost sea, meaning the Mediterranean Sea west of Jerusalem. They were going to die and lay in heaps and rot and stink under the sun because of the great things, meaning the devastating damage they had done in the land.

Does this apply to bugs? Yes, but the application, based on the rest of Scripture, can certainly cast a much wider net. Throughout the Bible, this type of an end is prophesied for any and all who come against Abraham's seed.

Joel 2:21 *Fear not, O land; be glad and rejoice: for the LORD will do great things.*

Joel gave the reminder that he, the locusts, had done great things, but the LORD, Jehovah, will do great things. Those great things to rectify the awful things had not yet been done. But since the promise had been given, everyone was to lay aside their fear and be glad and rejoice.

When the Lord writes a check, it never bounces.

Joel 2:22 *Be not afraid, ye beasts of the field: for the pastures of the wilderness do spring, for the tree beareth her fruit, the fig tree and the vine do yield their strength.*

This was Joel under the inspiration of the Holy Ghost, still speaking of a future promise in terms of a present certainty. The beasts of the field, which we have already seen languishing earlier in the book, are commanded not to be afraid. As far as God was concerned, the burned pastures of the wilderness were already springing up, the tree was already bearing the fruit, and the fig tree and the vine were already flexing their strength to bring forth their sweet produce.

Joel 2:23 *Be glad then, ye children of Zion, and rejoice in the LORD your God: for he hath given you the former rain moderately, and he will cause to come down for you the rain, the former rain, and the latter rain in the first month.*

The promises of God as a cause for joy continue in this verse. Joel commands the people to rejoice because *he hath given you the former rain moderately, and he will cause to come down for you the rain, the former rain, and the latter rain in the first month.*

Let me give you a bit of a timeline in this verse based on the wording used. The invasion of the locusts was a summertime thing when all of the crops were flourishing in the field. So, Joel, in the heat of the summer when everything had been devastated and everyone was starving, first of all, commanded the people to rejoice because God had assured that the former rain was coming moderately. And while we use the word former to mean something that has passed, and sometimes in Scripture it does mean that, this particular word in this place is a title for the rains that would fall from October to December. This was going to be the first thing needed to get their fields and crops reestablished.

As for the word *moderately*, the word it comes from paints an absolutely glorious picture. It is the word *tsedaqah*, and it is usually translated as "righteousness" or "salvation." In this particular case, the reason God preserved it for us as *moderately* is because this will be a righteous or saving rain, meaning a rain that comes at just the right time and in just the right proportion, neither too little to make a dent nor too much to wash everything away.

After God sends that former rain, Joel almost sounds like he is getting repetitive when he isn't. He says *and he will cause to come down for you the rain, the former rain, and the latter rain in the first month.*

The rain after that *former rain* in October through December refers to the needed rain showers that popped up from time to time after those rains. The latter rain at the end of this verse refers to the rains that fell in the springtime from March to April to get all of the crops moving towards full ripeness and maturity. And by using *the former rain* again just before speaking of the latter rain, he was pointing to the fact that when the next October through December rolled around, the needed rains in their season would still be coming.

Joel 2:24 *And the floors shall be full of wheat, and the fats shall overflow with wine and oil.*

The double use of the word *shall* in this verse confirms for us that everything Joel has been describing was a future promise so sure as to be referred to as an already present certainty. The barren floors of the barns were once again going to be full of wheat, and the fats, another word for a vat or a press, were going to overflow with wine from the grape and oil from the olive.

Joel 2:25 *And I will restore to you the years that the locust hath eaten, the cankerworm, and the caterpiller, and the palmerworm, my great army which I sent among you.*

This verse is often applied to the lives of those who have been wrecked and to the fact that God can restore all that has been lost through the years, and rightfully so. God was promising not to turn back the *clock* of the years but to turn back the *circumstances* of the years. He was promising to make up the deficit of all that had been eaten and restore it as thoroughly as if they had lost nothing.

No one has the restorative power of our God!

Joel 2:26 *And ye shall eat in plenty, and be satisfied, and praise the name of the LORD your God, that hath dealt wondrously with you: and my people shall never be ashamed.*

The scene and setting are still the Temple courtyard. Everyone can look down upon the land from there and behold devastation as far as the eye can see. But in response to the promises of God, Joel looks at these hungry people and gives this message from the LORD: *ye shall eat in plenty, and be satisfied, and praise the name of the LORD your God, that hath dealt wondrously with you: and my people shall never be ashamed.*

This is in response to the repentance of His people. God restores and rebuilds and forgives and blesses and removes humiliation based on the repentance of His people.

Joel 2:27 *And ye shall know that I am in the midst of Israel, and that I am the LORD your God, and none else: and my people shall never be ashamed.*

When the plague of the locusts was upon them, there would have been legitimate questions in the minds of the people as to whether Jehovah God was among them and whether or not He was still their God. By His full restoration of His impoverished people, that question would be put to rest; He is indeed the LORD their God, and none else, meaning "there is no other."

As for the last phrase in verse twenty-seven, you likely have noticed that it is the exact same as the last phrase in verse twenty-six. This is not some careless mistake or mindless repetition; the doubling of the promise is like a padlock securing it in place and guaranteeing it forever. God's people who return to Him in repentance will not be ashamed; they will forever find Him willing and able to restore them to a joyful fellowship with Him.

An afterward to consider

Joel 2:28 *And it shall come to pass afterward, that I will pour out my spirit upon all flesh; and your sons and your daughters shall prophesy, your old men shall dream dreams, your young men shall see visions:* **29** *And also upon the servants and upon the handmaids in those days will I pour out my spirit.*

All of Joel 2:28-32 is also found elsewhere in Scripture, and the other reference is far more well-known than this, the original reference. Peter quoted all of these last five verses of Joel 2 on the day of Pentecost:

Acts 2:17 *And it shall come to pass in the last days, saith God, I will pour out of my Spirit upon all flesh: and your sons and your daughters shall prophesy, and your young men shall see visions, and your old men shall dream dreams:* **18** *And on my servants and on my handmaidens I will pour out in those days of my Spirit; and they shall prophesy:* **19** *And I will shew wonders in heaven above, and signs in the earth beneath; blood, and fire, and vapour of smoke:* **20** *The sun shall be turned into darkness, and the moon into blood, before that great and notable day of the Lord come:* **21** *And it shall come to pass, that whosoever shall call on the name of the Lord shall be saved.*

All of Joel 2:28-29 was fulfilled during the time period of the book of Acts. God did pour out His Spirit upon all flesh, starting with the day of Pentecost and proceeding into all of the Gentile world. Both young men (Acts 19:6; 21:10) and young women (Acts 21:9) did prophesy. People had divine dreams and saw visions. God repeatedly poured out His Spirit on His servants.

And Joel saw all of this ahead of time as God was giving him both comfort for the present and a prophecy of the future that sprang off the calamity they had just come through.

Joel 2:30 *And I will shew wonders in the heavens and in the earth, blood, and fire, and pillars of smoke.* **31** *The sun shall be turned into darkness, and the moon into blood, before the great and the terrible day of the LORD come.*

Joel is now firmly looking ahead in time, past even the time of Peter and the book of Acts. These words apply to the Tribulation Period, and especially to a portion of it right before the LORD returns to this earth in judgment, which is here referred to as the terrible day of the LORD.

Wonders in Heaven and Earth? Here is a sampling:

Revelation 7:1 *And after these things I saw four angels standing on the four corners of the earth, holding the four winds of the earth, that the wind should not blow on the earth, nor on the sea, nor on any tree.*

Revelation 8:5 *And the angel took the censer, and filled it with fire of the altar, and cast it into the earth: and there were voices, and thunderings, and lightnings, and an earthquake.*

Blood and fire and pillars of smoke?

Revelation 8:7 *The first angel sounded, and there followed hail and fire mingled with blood, and they were cast upon the earth: and the third part of trees was burnt up, and all green grass was burnt up.* **8** *And the second angel sounded, and* *as it were a great mountain burning with fire was cast into the sea: and the third part of the sea became blood;*

The sun turned into darkness and the moon into blood?

Revelation 8:12 *And the fourth angel sounded, and the third part of the sun was smitten, and the third part of the moon, and the third part of the stars; so as the third part of them was darkened, and the day shone not for a third part of it, and the night likewise.*

Revelation 9:2 *And he opened the bottomless pit; and there arose a smoke out of the pit, as the smoke of a great furnace; and the sun and the air were darkened by reason of the smoke of the pit.*

Revelation 6:12 *And I beheld when he had opened the sixth seal, and, lo, there was a great earthquake; and the sun became black as sackcloth of hair, and the moon became as blood;*

We have not seen it yet—but Joel saw it all.

But he also saw this:

Joel 2:32 *And it shall come to pass, that whosoever shall call on the name of the LORD shall be delivered: for in mount Zion and in Jerusalem shall be deliverance, as the LORD hath said, and in the remnant whom the LORD shall call.*

If you are a Christian and/or have been raised in church, these words should sound very familiar to you. Only you likely know them from the New Testament and in a completely different context:

Romans 10:13 *For whosoever shall call upon the name of the Lord shall be saved.*

Joel's words in his day most properly applied to the prophecy of the Tribulation Period and of the fact that whoever of God's people, speaking of Israel, would call out to God, they would be delivered. That fits with the calamity they were experiencing in Joel's day, and it certainly fits with everything we read in the Book of the Revelation.

But the penmen of Scripture, under the inspiration of God, also applied it to salvation in our day through the Lord Jesus Christ.

The Jews of Joel's day would experience a great deliverance from the locusts, even though it all seemed hopeless as they examined the devastation around them.

The Jews of latter days will experience great deliverance from the Antichrist, even though it will look hopeless as they see nothing but enemies all around them.

Anyone at all of our day can experience a great deliverance from eternity in Hell, even though it seems hopeless as we see how wicked we are in the sight of God and how powerful the flesh and the devil and the world really are.

The LORD really will do great things!

Chapter Four
The Valley Of Decision

Joel 3:1 *For, behold, in those days, and in that time, when I shall bring again the captivity of Judah and Jerusalem,* **2** *I will also gather all nations, and will bring them down into the valley of Jehoshaphat, and will plead with them there for my people and for my heritage Israel, whom they have scattered among the nations, and parted my land.* **3** *And they have cast lots for my people; and have given a boy for an harlot, and sold a girl for wine, that they might drink.* **4** *Yea, and what have ye to do with me, O Tyre, and Zidon, and all the coasts of Palestine? will ye render me a recompence? and if ye recompense me, swiftly and speedily will I return your recompence upon your own head;* **5** *Because ye have taken my silver and my gold, and have carried into your temples my goodly pleasant things:* **6** *The children also of Judah and the children of Jerusalem have ye sold unto the Grecians, that ye might remove them far from their border.* **7** *Behold, I will raise them out of the place whither ye have sold them, and will return your recompence upon your own head:* **8** *And I will sell your sons and your daughters into the hand of the children of Judah, and they shall sell them to the Sabeans, to a people far off: for the LORD hath spoken it.* **9** *Proclaim ye this among the Gentiles; Prepare war, wake up the mighty men, let all the men of war draw near; let them come up:* **10** *Beat your plowshares into swords, and your pruninghooks* *into spears: let the weak say, I am strong.* **11** *Assemble yourselves, and come, all ye heathen, and gather yourselves together round about: thither cause thy mighty ones to come down, O LORD.* **12** *Let the heathen be wakened, and come up to the valley of Jehoshaphat: for there will I sit to judge all the heathen round about.* **13** *Put ye in the sickle, for the harvest is ripe: come, get you down; for the press is full, the fats overflow; for their wickedness is great.* **14** *Multitudes, multitudes in the valley of decision: for the day of the LORD is near in the valley of decision.* **15** *The sun and the moon shall be darkened, and the stars shall withdraw their shining.* **16** *The LORD also shall roar out of Zion, and utter his voice from Jerusalem; and the heavens and the earth shall shake: but the LORD will be the hope of his people, and the strength of the children of Israel.* **17** *So shall ye know that I am the LORD your God dwelling in Zion, my holy mountain: then shall Jerusalem be holy, and there shall no strangers pass through her any more.* **18** *And it shall come to pass in that day, that the mountains shall drop down new wine, and the hills shall flow with milk, and all the rivers of Judah shall flow with waters, and a fountain shall come forth of the house of the LORD, and shall water the valley of Shittim.* **19** *Egypt shall be a desolation, and Edom shall be a desolate wilderness, for the violence against the children of Judah, because they have shed innocent blood in their land.* **20** *But Judah shall dwell for ever, and Jerusalem from generation to generation.* **21** *For I will cleanse their blood that I have not cleansed: for the LORD dwelleth in Zion.*

Locusts had descended upon the land and devoured everything in sight. And this was such an out-of-the-ordinary-sized plague of locusts that Joel knew it was a supernatural occurrence rather than a natural occurrence. The people were under the judgment of God for their behavior.

Joel used all of this to point ahead in time to the day of the LORD, primarily speaking of the Tribulation Period and the even more devastating judgment it would bring.

And in chapter three, that will be the heavy focus. God has already dealt with the bugs—now He will deal with the pests.

A pleading in the valley

Joel 3:1 *For, behold, in those days, and in that time, when I shall bring again the captivity of Judah and Jerusalem, 2 I will also gather all nations, and will bring them down into the valley of Jehoshaphat, and will plead with them there for my people and for my heritage Israel, whom they have scattered among the nations, and parted my land.*

Remember that throughout the short book of Joel, while he has been dealing with the present calamity of the locusts, he has been doing so with an eye toward a future and greater calamity, the Tribulation Period. So he has been looking ahead—far ahead—to a time still yet future even to us, though likely not too very far away in our day.

In that context, as Joel chapter three begins, God says, *For, behold, in those days, and in that time, when I shall bring again the captivity of Judah and Jerusalem...*

Here, in our twenty-first-century perch, we can now look *back on* what Joel was looking *ahead to* in these words. We have the luxury of a clear historical view rather than the somewhat veiled prophetical view.

Israel was expelled from her land in A.D. 136 after the Bar Kochba rebellion of A.D. 132-135. For the better part of 1,800 years that followed, they were *wanderers among the nations*. Nations like Spain. Nations like Germany. Nations that despised them and were determined to destroy them. It would not be until 1948 that they once again had their own land.

This verse in Joel has that restoration and the years that follow in view. But as we get into verse two, things move even further ahead in time to a coming climactic battle:

Joel 3:2 *I will also gather all nations, and will bring them down into the valley of Jehoshaphat, and will plead with them there for my people and for my heritage Israel, whom they have scattered among the nations, and parted my land.*

We should, first of all, examine a location given to us in these words, the valley of Jehoshaphat. It is only called by that name twice in Scripture, both of them right here in Joel chapter three; and under that name, it harkens back to a great slaughter made against the Ammonites and Moabites in 2 Chronicles 20:22-26.

In verse fourteen, it will be referred to by another name, the valley of decision.

But you almost assuredly know it by a very different and much more ominous name: Armageddon.

What we read here in Joel 3 matches what we read about in Revelation 14 and Revelation 16. In Revelation 16:16, we are actually given the name Armageddon:

Revelation 16:16 *And he gathered them together into a place called in the Hebrew tongue Armageddon.*

In Revelation 14, speaking of the great battle that will take place at Armageddon, we find this:

Revelation 14:19 *And the angel thrust in his sickle into the earth, and gathered the vine of the earth, and cast it into the great winepress of the wrath of God.* **20** *And the winepress was trodden without the city, and blood came out of the winepress, even unto the horse bridles, by the space of a thousand and six hundred furlongs.*

Here in Joel, we find the same:

Joel 3:12 *Let the heathen be wakened, and come up to the valley of Jehoshaphat: for there will I sit to judge all the* *heathen round about.* **13** *Put ye in the sickle, for the harvest is ripe: come, get you down; for the press is full, the fats overflow; for their wickedness is great.*

We could go on at extensive length showing the parallels in these two passages; the Valley of Jehoshaphat is the Valley of Decision is Armageddon. And God said that in that place He *will also gather all nations, and will bring them down into the valley of Jehoshaphat, and will plead with them there for my people and for my heritage Israel, whom they have scattered among the nations, and parted my land.*

God is going to bring all the nations that have hated Israel so badly into this valley and utterly wreck them. To *plead* in this verse means nothing like our modern concept of whining and begging; it is from the word *shaphat*, and it means to enter into a controversy.

Just as in Joel 2:17, God once again in Joel 3:2 refers to Israel as His heritage; a person would be safer jumping into a running woodchipper than aligning themselves with the antisemites of the world.

God accused the nations of scattering His people and partitioning off His land. And that is exactly what happened; we still see the results of that in real time in our day. So, for all of this, God will draw the nations of the world into the valley for a confrontation.

A people being trafficked

Joel 3:3 *And they have cast lots for my people; and have given a boy for an harlot, and sold a girl for wine, that they might drink.*

Joel now brings things a bit nearer to his own day, yet still prophetical to his. Both Obadiah and Nahum mention instances like what we are reading about here. When Israel began to fall, nations around her, nations like Edom and Assyria, reduced the individual people of Israel to cheap pieces of property. They gambled for them, they traded little boys as payment for a night with prostitutes, and they sold little girls to get money for booze.

This was God's heritage; this would not end well.

Joel 3:4 *Yea, and what have ye to do with me, O Tyre, and Zidon, and all the coasts of Palestine? will ye render me a recompence? and if ye recompense me, swiftly and speedily will I return your recompence upon your own head;* **5** *Because ye have taken my silver and my gold, and have carried into your temples my goodly pleasant things:* **6** *The children also of Judah and the children of Jerusalem have ye sold unto the Grecians, that ye might remove them far from their border.*

God names three places/people groups that He was angry with in this verse, and one of them is historically significant in our day, so we will deal with it first. It is the name Palestine, and this is the only place it is found in Scripture.

Many world maps today have Palestine on them, right where Israel is. When Israel was cast out of her land, the Romans renamed it Palestine as an insult to the Jews. We still hear newscasts today speaking of Palestine and the Palestinian people. A popular antisemitic chant that has been used a great deal in the 2020s is "From the river to the sea, Palestine shall be free." That chant is a call for genocide against the Jewish people.

But please notice here that Palestine was not Israel; Palestine was a place on the Mediterranean seacoast whose people would be coming against Israel. Palestine comes from the word for Philistine, the ancient and inveterate enemies of Israel.

Tyre and Zidon, elsewhere spelled Sidon, were Phoenician cities further up North on the Mediterranean seacoast.

So, God here mentions His anger toward Tyre, Sidon, and the Philistines for what they will be doing to His people. In speaking of that, He says *will ye render me a recompence? and if ye recompense me, swiftly and speedily will I return your recompence upon your own head;*

In our terms, this was God saying, "Do you intend to retaliate against Me by coming against My people? Bring it, but be ready, because I am immediately going to bring it right back to you."

God's next accusation against the enemies of His people was, *...ye have taken my silver and my gold, and have carried into your temples my goodly pleasant things:*

Examples of this from history are too numerous to mention, and God's people were not spared this indignity. In 2 Chronicles 21:16-17, the Philistines and Arabians carried off all the treasures of King Jehoram's house. In 2 Kings 14:13-13, Jehoash of Israel took all of the treasures both of the king's house and the LORD's house in Judah to Samaria. As we famously read in the book of Daniel, Nebuchadnezzar took the gold and silver vessels from the Temple of God in Jerusalem to Babylon.

In verse six, God levels a new accusation, saying, *The children also of Judah and the children of Jerusalem have ye sold unto the Grecians, that ye might remove them far from their border.*

This is the first time we find any form of the English word "Greek" or "Grecian" in the Bible. But we find them under another name in Ezekiel, and that reference mentions what God is describing here:

Ezekiel 27:13 *<u>Javan</u>, Tubal, and Meshech, they were thy merchants: they traded the persons of men and vessels of brass in thy market.*

Javen is from the exact same word as the word "Grecian." The Javanites, who became better known as Grecians when they became a world power, trafficked in people. And knowing this, the enemies of Israel, particularly the Phoenicians of Tyre and Zidon, sold the Israelites that they captured to the far-off Grecians so that they could never make it home.

God took great exception to that:

Joel 3:7 *Behold, I will raise them out of the place whither ye have sold them, and will return your recompence upon your own head:* **8** *And I will sell your sons and your daughters into the hand of the children of Judah, and they shall sell them to the Sabeans, to a people far off: for the LORD hath spoken it.*

This is abundantly plain. God was going to raise His people up out of their far-off bondage and bring them home. Then He was going to turn His attention to some very serious recompense; or, in our words, payback. And that payback was going to be very exact and pointed. He was going to sell the children of Judah's enemies into their hands so that they could then sell them to the Sabeans, a *people far off*.

Her enemies sold her people into as far a land as they could; God was going to let Judah do the exact same to them. In later years, when Alexander the Great expanded Greece into a world power, he came against the Phoenicians and reduced them to slavery. The Jews then bought a bunch of them and sold them at a profit to the Sabeans, another word for Arabians.

A proclamation among the Gentiles

Joel 3:9 *Proclaim ye this among the Gentiles; Prepare war, wake up the mighty men, let all the men of war draw near; let them come up:* **10** *Beat your plowshares into swords, and your pruninghooks into spears: let the weak say, I am strong.*

In Scripture, God does a great deal of inviting; not all of it, though, is positive. In this case, it is decidedly negative. The Gentiles, people who had lined themselves up against His people, would be invited to a war—a war against God. And while this had several nearer-term applications in the years that shortly followed the prophecy of Joel, this mainly deals once again with the battle near the end of the Tribulation Period. It is then that, more than ever, the entire Gentile world will be gathered together against Israel and against God.

Thus, God tells the Gentiles, *Prepare war, wake up the mighty men, let all the men of war draw near; let them come up...*

There is a bit of not-so-thinly-veiled sarcasm from God in these words; He was picturing the mightiest men that the Gentiles have to offer as sleeping and in need of being awakened. God wants all of their men of war to draw near and come up; this battle is to be the one that finally and forever settles the issue at hand.

Further adding salt to the wound, He says, *Beat your plowshares into swords, and your pruninghooks into spears: let the weak say, I am strong.* In other words, their warriors have settled down as farmers and will need to reforge their farm implements into weapons. They have also let their muscles and might deteriorate through their placid lifestyle and must, therefore, pump themselves up, calling themselves strong even though they are weak.

Joel 3:11 *Assemble yourselves, and come, all ye heathen, and gather yourselves together round about: thither cause thy mighty ones to come down, O LORD.*

The voice changes in verse eleven. God had been speaking, and now Joel responds. He echoes God's invitation for the heathen to come to the battle and then implores God to make sure that all the mighty ones among the enemy do indeed make it there. God wants this matter settled—and Joel does as well.

As for the word heathen, although the English word has not yet been used in Joel 3, the word that it comes from has. It is from the word *goy,* and in verse nine, it is translated as Gentiles. It will be used twice more in the next verse.

Joel 3:12 *Let the heathen be wakened, and come up to the valley of Jehoshaphat: for there will I sit to judge all the heathen round about.*

God begins to speak again in verse twelve, answering Joel's request given in verse eleven. He commands the heathens, the enemy Gentiles, to wake up and come to the valley of Jehoshaphat. And His purpose is not to see who will win the battle; that is already pre-decided in any contest where one of the combatants is named "God."

He is bringing them to that valley to judge them.

A press overflowing

Joel 3:13 *Put ye in the sickle, for the harvest is ripe: come, get you down; for the press is full, the fats overflow; for their wickedness is great.*

Normally, when people in those days spoke of a ripe harvest and a full press and overflowing fats, it was a very good and exciting thing. All of these terms spoke of grape vines that were loaded with grapes, and all of the grapes so loaded with juice that they were about to burst. It spoke of people gathering those grapes, putting them in the winepress, treading them out, and gathering the juice.

The thing that made this reference to all of that a deadly and ominous thing is that it was not grapes being spoken of but people, and not juice, but the wickedness in those people. God intended to cut them down as with a sickle and stomp on them until they were utterly crushed.

Joel 3:14 *Multitudes, multitudes in the valley of decision: for the day of the LORD is near in the valley of decision.*

When we speak of the valley of decision, it is usually taken the wrong way entirely. It is normally pictured as a place where people have a hard choice to make, and we hope they will make the right one. But in this case, the only One making any decision in the valley of decision is God. Everyone else has already made their choice, else they would not be there. All of the multitudes are now waiting on the decision of God, which refers back to the judgment He promised in verse twelve.

Joel's doubled usage of *multitudes* in this verse gives us a bare sense of how vast the assembly will be. But it would take John the Beloved several hundred years later to give a clearer sense of the enormity of the crowd:

Revelation 14:19 *And the angel thrust in his sickle into the earth, and gathered the vine of the earth, and cast it into the great winepress of the wrath of God.* **20** *And the winepress was trodden without the city, and blood came out of the winepress, even unto the horse bridles, by the space of a thousand and six hundred furlongs.*

Based on these numbers, the blood is going to flow some four feet deep in the center of the valley, and the flow will run for 1600 furlongs, which works out to about 200 miles. No wonder Joel said *multitudes, multitudes*.

A picture of the future

Joel 3:15 *The sun and the moon shall be darkened, and the stars shall withdraw their shining.*

Once again, we find Joel writing of things that John later gave us much more details on in the Book of the Revelation:

Revelation 8:12 *And the fourth angel sounded, and the third part of the sun was smitten, and the third part of the moon, and the third part of the stars; so as the third part of them was darkened, and the day shone not for a third part of it, and the night likewise.*

Exactly one-third of the sun will be smitten and will not shine during the day. Exactly one-third of the moon will be smitten and will not shine at night. Exactly one-third of the stars will simply go out and not give off any light.

Because of the damage to the sun, moon, and stars, when there is light, it will be an eerie two-thirds light. Imagine the weird feeling when there is only two-thirds of the normal light, day and night. Additionally, there will be no light at all for a third of normal daylight hours, or for a third of normal nighttime hours.

Joel 3:16 *The LORD also shall roar out of Zion, and utter his voice from Jerusalem; and the heavens and the earth shall shake: but the LORD will be the hope of his people, and the strength of the children of Israel.*

One of the most despised words in our world today is anything to do with Zion or Zionism. One of the most despised concepts is the idea that the Jews are God's special, chosen people, as far as nations go. But both of these things are Biblical, and they are seen together in this verse.

When Jesus came the first time, He came as a Lamb, and in the words of Isaiah 53:7, faced affliction and opened not His mouth. But when He, Jehovah/Jesus, comes again, it will be as the Lion of the Tribe of Judah (Revelation 5:5). And though He will still be every bit the Lamb that was slain (Revelation 5:6), He will also, in the words of Joel, *roar out of Zion, and utter his voice from Jerusalem,* with the result being that *the heavens and the earth shall shake.* To His embattled people, *the LORD will be the hope of his people, and the strength of the children of Israel.*

Joel 3:17 *So shall ye know that I am the LORD your God dwelling in Zion, my holy mountain: then shall Jerusalem be holy, and there shall no strangers pass through her any more.*

When Jehovah personally and physically sits on the throne in Jerusalem during the Millennial Reign, for that is what is now being spoken of, no strangers will so much as pass through that holy place. In this, though, we need to do some comparing and some defining to get an accurate picture of what is being said.

On the defining end, the word stranger is from *zoor,* and it indicates one who is immoral, loathsome, and an enemy. So, this is not merely someone who is not a Jew; this is one who is not a Jew and who is antagonistic to the Jews and to the one true God.

On the comparing end, notice what the prophet Zechariah said:

Zechariah 14:16 *And it shall come to pass, that every one that is left of all the nations which came against Jerusalem shall even go up from year to year to worship the King, the LORD of hosts, and to keep the feast of tabernacles.*

Joel said no stranger would be there. Zechariah said, *every one that is left of all the nations which came against Jerusalem shall even go up from year to year to worship the King*. Tied together, we clearly see that God is promising that Jerusalem will be open to *all* peoples, but *only* to those of them who love God and the Jews.

Never again will Jerusalem be trodden down by the Gentiles.

Joel 3:18 *And it shall come to pass in that day, that the mountains shall drop down new wine, and the hills shall flow with milk, and all the rivers of Judah shall flow with waters, and a fountain shall come forth of the house of the LORD, and shall water the valley of Shittim.*

These verses are very clearly referring to and describing the Millennial Reign of Christ. But, please remember that as Joel spoke and wrote these things to his people, they were still looking for a near-term fulfillment of them since they had just been devastated by the plague of locusts.

But, as a description of the Millennial Reign, we find everything in and around Jerusalem in a perfect and prosperous state. Within the description of that, though, we find the supernatural mixed in with the natural. Here are the words again:

Joel 3:18 *And it shall come to pass in that day, that the mountains shall drop down new wine, and the hills shall flow with milk, and all the rivers of Judah shall flow with waters, <u>and a fountain shall come forth of the house of the LORD, and shall water the valley of Shittim</u>.*

Here is where we find this elsewhere in Scripture, both during the Millennial Reign and in the new Heaven and new Earth, Jerusalem, and the new Jerusalem:

Zechariah 14:8 *And it shall be in that day, that living waters shall go out from Jerusalem; half of them toward the former sea, and half of them toward the hinder sea: in summer and in winter shall it be.*

Revelation 22:1 *And he shewed me a pure river of water of life, clear as crystal, proceeding out of the throne of God and of the Lamb.*

God will have a river, sourced from His throne, watering His land!

Please keep in mind that Joel is describing the thousand-year Millennial Reign of Christ. You need to understand that as you begin to look at the next verse:

Joel 3:19 *Egypt shall be a desolation, and Edom shall be a desolate wilderness, for the violence against the children of Judah, because they have shed innocent blood in their land.*

Through the years, people have often gotten a wrong view of the early days of the Millennial Reign. They believe that as soon as Jesus returns after the Tribulation Period, all of the flowers instantly lose their thorns, the atmosphere immediately purifies to celestial air, and there is no trace at all of the ravages of sin on our planet.

But that is not at all the case. Remember, please, that there will be both lost and saved, both eternal and temporal, in the Millennial Reign. Not everyone on earth will die during the Tribulation Period because not everyone was old enough or able enough to go to war at Armageddon. So lost people will find themselves in the Millennial Reign of Christ, and their population will increase through the thousand years to the point that the devil will find a great multitude willing to follow him into one last battle against God in Revelation 20:7-8.

These lost people who enter the Millennial Reign will need to see with their eyes the results of being the enemy of God and of His people. Egypt and Edom (modern-day Jordan) will have been the particular enemies of Israel during the Tribulation Period and will face the equally particular ire of God. So, while the earth begins to heal to an Edenic state during the thousand years, the slowest places to heal will be Egypt and Edom. And in Egypt's case, we are actually given a time period for their desolation elsewhere in Scripture:

Ezekiel 29:12 *And I will make the land of Egypt desolate in the midst of the countries that are desolate, and her cities among the cities that are laid waste shall be desolate forty years: and I will scatter the Egyptians among the nations, and will disperse them through the countries.* **13** *Yet thus saith the Lord GOD; At the end of forty years will I gather the Egyptians from the people whither they were scattered:* **14** *And I will bring again the captivity of Egypt, and will cause them to return into the land of Pathros, into the land of their habitation; and they shall be there a base kingdom.* **15** *It shall be the basest of the kingdoms; neither shall it exalt itself any more above the nations: for I will diminish them, that they shall no more rule over the nations.*

Egypt will spend the first forty years of the Millennial Reign as the basest of nations, desolate and slowly recovering.

Joel 3:20 *But Judah shall dwell for ever, and Jerusalem from generation to generation.*

This is yet another of the many verses in Scripture that make Replacement Theology look foolish. The church is precious to God; the most precious of all, in fact. But the Jews are also still precious to God, and the church is not them and will not replace them. Judah will dwell forever, and Jerusalem from generation to generation.

Joel 3:21 *For I will cleanse their blood that I have not cleansed: for the LORD dwelleth in Zion.*

Those espousing Replacement Theology usually teach that the Jews got so dirty and sinful, especially in bringing about the crucifixion of Christ, that God decided to do away with them and replace them with us. Never mind that we have been every bit, and more so, sinful than them; the claim must simply be believed because it is said. But, the very last verse of Joel makes it clear that though God has not cleansed them, He will cleanse them. And this is rooted in the promise *for the LORD dwelleth in Zion*.

Not America: Zion. Not the United Kingdom: Zion. Not Rome: Zion. Definitely not in the assembly of any of the antisemites in lands all across the globe: Zion.

No insects will ever remove or replace God's people, nor will any pests.

Amos
Turmoil In Damascus, Gaza, Tyre, Edom, Ammon, Moab, Judah, And Israel

Chapter Five
The Shepherd and The Wolves

Amos 1:1 *The words of Amos, who was among the herdmen of Tekoa, which he saw concerning Israel in the days of Uzziah king of Judah, and in the days of Jeroboam the son of Joash king of Israel, two years before the earthquake.* **2** *And he said, The LORD will roar from Zion, and utter his voice from Jerusalem; and the habitations of the shepherds shall mourn, and the top of Carmel shall wither.* **3** *Thus saith the LORD; For three transgressions of Damascus, and for four, I will not turn away the punishment thereof; because they have threshed Gilead with threshing instruments of iron:* **4** *But I will send a fire into the house of Hazael, which shall devour the palaces of Benhadad.* **5** *I will break also the bar of Damascus, and cut off the inhabitant from the plain of Aven, and him that holdeth the sceptre from the house of Eden: and the people of Syria shall go into captivity unto Kir, saith the LORD.* **6** *Thus saith the LORD; For three transgressions of Gaza, and for four, I will not turn away the punishment thereof; because they carried away captive the whole captivity, to deliver them up to Edom:* **7** *But I will send a fire on the wall of Gaza, which shall devour the palaces thereof:* **8** *And I will cut off the inhabitant from Ashdod, and him that holdeth the sceptre from Ashkelon, and I will turn mine hand against Ekron: and the remnant of the Philistines shall perish, saith the Lord GOD.* **9** *Thus saith the LORD; For three* *transgressions of Tyrus, and for four, I will not turn away the punishment thereof; because they delivered up the whole captivity to Edom, and remembered not the brotherly covenant:* **10** *But I will send a fire on the wall of Tyrus, which shall devour the palaces thereof.* **11** *Thus saith the LORD; For three transgressions of Edom, and for four, I will not turn away the punishment thereof; because he did pursue his brother with the sword, and did cast off all pity, and his anger did tear perpetually, and he kept his wrath for ever:* **12** *But I will send a fire upon Teman, which shall devour the palaces of Bozrah.* **13** *Thus saith the LORD; For three transgressions of the children of Ammon, and for four, I will not turn away the punishment thereof; because they have ripped up the women with child of Gilead, that they might enlarge their border:* **14** *But I will kindle a fire in the wall of Rabbah, and it shall devour the palaces thereof, with shouting in the day of battle, with a tempest in the day of the whirlwind:* **15** *And their king shall go into captivity, he and his princes together, saith the LORD.*

The old hillbilly preacher was looked upon with disdain as soon as he entered the ministry. The polished pastors with their seminary degrees quickly deemed him as unqualified for the task; after all, his clothing was tattered and his shoes were never shined, and no one before him in his family had ever been a preacher.

He had rarely ever been to the big city. His fingernails usually had dirt under them from his farming activity, whereas theirs were always clean and soft from their consistent clerical lifestyle. See, he not only kept livestock, he also worked the ground.

Who did this illiterate hick think he was, anyway, invading their sacred space?

His name was Amos. And as everyone was quick to learn, especially those professional prophets, the "hillbilly" was actually brilliant, eloquent, and powerful both in his preaching and his personality.

The background in question

Amos 1:1 *The words of Amos, who was among the herdmen of Tekoa, which he saw concerning Israel in the days of Uzziah king of Judah, and in the days of Jeroboam the son of Joash king of Israel, two years before the earthquake.*

The only place in Scripture we find this Amos is right here in the book that bears his name. There is one other Amos mentioned in the genealogy of Christ in Luke 3, but he seems likely to have been separated from this Amos by a few hundred years or so. In these opening words of his prophecy, we find the general time period in which he lived and the occupation in which he was employed. He was a contemporary of the prophet Hosea, ministering during the days of Uzziah and Jeroboam II as Hosea did. He lived fairly early in the period of the divided kingdom.

His prophecy came to him two years before the earthquake. We do not have a date for this earthquake, but it was so severe and so significant that Zechariah also mentioned it two centuries later:

Zechariah 14:5 *And ye shall flee to the valley of the mountains; for the valley of the mountains shall reach unto Azal: yea, ye shall flee, <u>like as ye fled from before the earthquake in the days of Uzziah king of Judah</u>: and the LORD my God shall come, and all the saints with thee.*

When you see things like this, it should help you to remember that the Bible is a history book. These details and dates and names and places defy the silly notion that the Bible is mythology rather than an account of what has been and what will be.

As we see in the book of Hosea, this time period was very prosperous for everyone economically; the Northern Kingdom was now at the height of its power and wealth. And that means that Amos's message of coming judgment was every bit as despised as Hosea's message of coming judgment.

As to occupation, we find here that Amos was of the herdsmen of Tekoa. Amos was from Judah, the Southern Kingdom. Tekoa was six miles south of Bethlehem in a rugged yet beautiful region of the land. Amos really was "from the sticks" in our vernacular. He tended sheep out there in Tekoa. As we will find in chapter seven of the book, he was also employed in gathering sycamore fruit.

There was simply nothing about the background of Amos that would have led anyone to surmise he might end up being a powerful prophet of God. And yet, that is exactly what God made of him. And even though he was from Judah, God made him a prophet to Israel – a fact that was going to cause great contention that we will see later on in the book. It would be much akin to a country preacher from lower Alabama making his way to New York City to tell all of the "big-city folk" how unhappy God is with them.

But if Israel was upset with that message, they would soon find themselves with a lot of company. While Joel merely prophesied of turmoil in Judah, Amos was going to thunder of the judgment of God on pretty much everybody, starting with Damascus and then going on to Gaza, Tyre, Edom, Ammon, Moab, Judah, and then really settling in on Israel.

The beginning of the message

Amos 1:2 *And he said, The LORD will roar from Zion, and utter his voice from Jerusalem; and the habitations of the shepherds shall mourn, and the top of Carmel shall wither.*

Just seven verses earlier in the text of Scripture, we find the LORD roaring from Zion:

Joel 3:16 *The LORD also shall roar out of Zion, and utter his voice from Jerusalem; and the heavens and the earth shall shake: but the LORD will be the hope of his people, and the strength of the children of Israel.*

The difference between these two "roarings" of the LORD from Zion is that it was an encouraging roaring at the end of the book of Joel and is an ominous roaring as Amos begins his prophecy. And what made it ominous, at least from Israel's perspective, was that God had been roaring for them previously and would now be heard to roar against them.

The result of that roaring would be that *the habitations of the shepherds shall mourn, and the top of Carmel shall wither.*

Carmel was prime Israeli real estate, maybe the nicest and most verdant in the entire land. It overlooked the Mediterranean Sea, had fantastic pastureland, and was perfect for the cultivation of olives and grapes. The point of calling out Carmel right here at the beginning, as Feinberg points out, is this: "if Caramel withers, how great will be the desolation elsewhere?" (Feinberg, 87)

This is the abrupt manner and wording with which Amos began his prophecy.

The broadness of the strokes

Amos 1:3 *Thus saith the LORD; For three transgressions of Damascus, and for four, I will not turn away the punishment thereof; because they have threshed Gilead with threshing instruments of iron:* **4** *But I will send a fire into the house of Hazael, which shall devour the palaces of Benhadad.*

Eight times in the book of Amos, you are going to find the poetic figure of speech Amos loves to utilize: "For three transgressions and for four." And you should have no trouble figuring out that these were not intended to be looked upon as dry factual math; they were intended to be used for poetic emphasis in the same way that we say something like, "If I've told you once, I've told you a thousand times."

This three-then-four formula is designed to picture their transgressions as infinite, in other words.

Damascus is first on the list. Damascus was the capital city of Syria and was 140 miles northeast of Jerusalem. God cast His eye of judgment onto that far city and said that He would not pardon them for their transgressions. And their transgressions, as He quickly specifies, were that they had *threshed Gilead with threshing instruments of iron.*

Gilead was the Israeli territory on the eastern side of the Jordan River. Because of that, it was an easy and prime target for Syria. And one of those Syrian kings, a wicked man named Hazael, committed a horrible atrocity against the Jews in Gilead:

2 Kings 13:7 *Neither did he leave of the people to Jehoahaz but fifty horsemen, and ten chariots, and ten thousand footmen; for the king of Syria had destroyed them, and had made them like the dust <u>by threshing</u>.*

Threshing was used on grain to grind it down, and it was done by heavy iron sledges. A very firm surface would be used, and then those iron sledges could pound something into powder.

Hazael of Syria did this to people—God's people. It was not enough for him to conquer them, nor even to kill them; he had to disrespect and utterly denigrate them as he did.

And God did not take kindly to it. He said, *But I will send a fire into the house of Hazael, which shall devour the palaces of Benhadad.*

Benhadad was the son and heir of Hazael. In 2 Kings 14, God allowed Israel to regain her strength and wreck Syria because of what Hazael had done to them.

By the way, on the "the Bible is history, not mythology" front once again, there is in the British Museum a black marble obelisk found in the central palace of Nimroud, inscribed with the names of Hazael and Ben-hadad of Syria, as well as Jehu of Israel. (Jamieson, 2:528).

Amos 1:5 *I will break also the bar of Damascus, and cut off the inhabitant from the plain of Aven, and him that holdeth the sceptre from the house of Eden: and the people of Syria shall go into captivity unto Kir, saith the LORD.*

In his final word of judgment against Syria, God began by saying that He would break the bar of Damascus. That referred to the long traverse bars of the city gates that gave them their strength and kept the enemies at bay. God was promising to shatter those and allow their enemies in on them.

The Plain of Aven and the House of Eden were two areas in Syria, both part of the valley of Damascus. They were prime Syrian real estate and where many of the power brokers of the day resided. God used that place and that people as symbolic of all the land, saying, *and the people of Syria shall go into captivity unto Kir, saith the LORD.*

Kir was in Assyria; God was going to send the then-current scourge of the earth against Syria for what they did to His people.

Amos 1:6 *Thus saith the LORD; For three transgressions of Gaza, and for four, I will not turn away the punishment thereof; because they carried away captive the whole captivity, to deliver them up to Edom:*

Gaza was one of the five chief cities of the Philistines, and here in the prophecy of Amos, it is used as a descriptive term for all of Philistia, just like Damascus is used as a descriptive term for all of Syria.

God's indictment against the Philistines was that they *carried away captive the whole captivity, to deliver them up to*

Edom. At some point in history, and there are a few passages in the Old Testament that could potentially refer to this event, the Philistines took a large body of Jewish people captive. And rather than allowing any of them ever to return, or even to remain nearby, they sold them as a wholesale lot of humanity to the Edomites, the people who hated them worse than anyone else on earth.

This was nothing less than an attempted genocide, and therefore, God would in no way remove their punishment for it.

That punishment begins to be described for us in the next few verses:

Amos 1:7 *But I will send a fire on the wall of Gaza, which shall devour the palaces thereof:* **8** *And I will cut off the inhabitant from Ashdod, and him that holdeth the sceptre from Ashkelon, and I will turn mine hand against Ekron: and the remnant of the Philistines shall perish, saith the Lord GOD.*

In these verses, God mentions four out of the five of those primary Philistine cities: Gaza, Ashdod, Ashkelon, and Ekron. The only one not mentioned is Gath, which seems to have fallen at the hand of King Uzziah in 2 Chronicles 26:6.

The destruction that God describes in these verses is all-encompassing. The wall of Gaza, the very defense of the city, would be burned down. The palaces would also be decimated by that same fire. The regular citizens of Ashdod would be cut off. The king who was holding the scepter of power would be cut off from Ashkelon, and God would turn His hand entirely against Ekron. The result of all of this would be that the remnant of the Philistines would perish.

And if you want to know how that worked out, search for any form of the word Philistine after Zechariah 9:6.

You will not find any, not a single one. The race of the Philistines has been either exterminated or assimilated and is no more.

Amos 1:9 *Thus saith the LORD; For three transgressions of Tyrus, and for four, I will not turn away the punishment thereof; because they delivered up the whole captivity to Edom, and remembered not the brotherly covenant:*

Tyrus, Tyre, was the great capital of the Phoenician Empire, and here stands in for the Phoenician Empire in this prophecy and judgment. It was north of Israel, on the Mediterranean Sea, in what is now modern-day Lebanon.

As God lays out the case for His anger against them, He says that they *delivered up the whole captivity to Edom*. But then He points to a factor that made this even more egregious, saying that they *remembered not the brotherly covenant*.

At some point, the Phoenicians, like the Philistines that we just mentioned, captured a huge number of Jews. They then sold them wholesale to the Edomites, making sure that none could ever return. But in their past, there was indeed a brotherly covenant. That reference goes as far back as the days of David. King David of Israel and King Hiram of Tyre had been the best of friends, and that friendship continued into the days of Solomon. Hiram provided much of the material and many of the laborers to help David and Solomon build the Temple, their individual palaces, and their kingdom.

For their part, among other things, not a single king of Israel or Judah ever made war against the Phoenicians; they remembered that brotherly covenant.

And yet there came a day when the Phoenicians saw an opportunity to make a quick profit off of Jewish captives, and they did so without hesitation, regardless of the fact that they would be potentially participating in a genocide.

God's judgment would be swift and sure:

Amos 1:10 *But I will send a fire on the wall of Tyrus, which shall devour the palaces thereof.*

Some years later, Nebuchadnezzar and the Chaldeans came against Tyre. They besieged it for thirteen years, finally decimating it. It was later finished off entirely by Alexander the Great.

In 1828, Adam Clarke described it this way: "It is now only a place for a few poor fishermen to spread their nets upon." (Clarke, 4:673)

Amos 1:11 *Thus saith the LORD; For three transgressions of Edom, and for four, I will not turn away the punishment thereof; because he did pursue his brother with the sword, and did cast off all pity, and his anger did tear perpetually, and he kept his wrath for ever:*

We have already seen Edom mentioned offhandedly twice in the first chapter of the book of Amos; both of those mentions were about Edom buying Jewish captives from those who had taken them prisoners. Now, Edom will be mentioned directly.

God was angry with Edom because *he did pursue his brother with the sword, and did cast off all pity, and his anger did tear perpetually, and he kept his wrath for ever:*

The reference to Edom as Israel's brother is because they actually were brothers. Jacob and Esau became Israel and Edom, both in the names they were later given and in the nations that they became.

Although there was a partial and temporary reconciliation between Jacob and Esau, Esau never really did get over what Jacob did to him; the years only made it fester. As the generations followed, the two nations that came from those two brothers continued to be at odds.

The accusation God finally made against Edom was fourfold: *he did pursue his brother with the sword, and did cast off all pity, and his anger did tear perpetually, and he kept his wrath for ever:*

Jamiesson, Faussett, and Brown do a good job describing some of the history behind these four accusations, saying, "Edom first showed his spite in not letting Israel pass through his borders when coming from the wilderness, but threatening to come out against him with the sword; next, when the Syrians attacked Jerusalem under Ahaz (compare 2Ch 28:17; 2Ki 16:516:5); next, when Nebuchadnezzar assailed Jerusalem (Ps 137:7,8). In each case, Edom chose the day of Israel's calamity for venting his grudge." (Jamieson 2:530)

The words are so much more than just historical doings, though. Look at some of them again:

...cast off all pity, and his anger did tear perpetually, and he kept his wrath for ever:

That is a horrible description. These were people who hardened their hearts and held grudges and steamed and fumed every day of their miserable human existence. They would never allow themselves to be happy with what or who they had because that happiness may make them temporarily forget the hatred they wanted to harbor every moment of every day toward their own family. And the worst part is that all of the things they were so angry about were from generations long past, had nothing to do with anyone then living, and had not hindered their present success in any way. They were angry at the children of the children of the children (etc.) that hurt the fathers of the fathers of the fathers of their fathers.

People like that do not need any enemies whatsoever because they do a flawless job of destroying themselves without help from anyone. But they, Edom, did have an enemy nonetheless, namely the God who saw what they continually did to Israel:

Amos 1:12 *But I will send a fire upon Teman, which shall devour the palaces of Bozrah.*

Teman and Bozrah were two of the primary cities of Edom. Bozrah, in particular, was a strong and heavily fortified city. So, in promising to bring the ruin of those two cities, God was promising to wreck the entire land.

Amos 1:13 *Thus saith the LORD; For three transgressions of the children of Ammon, and for four, I will not turn away the punishment thereof; because they have ripped up the women with child of Gilead, that they might enlarge their border:*

Just like the Edomites, the Ammonites were related to Israel. Both Moab and Ammon came from the incestuous relationship of the daughters of Lot (nephew of Abraham) with their father. And yet, when Ammon saw a chance to expand their territory through the slaughter of the inhabitants of Gilead, they not only did so, but they did so with an unspeakable brutality that God describes in this verse. There was no need to murder pregnant women and babies; they did so for effect; they did so for mere cruelty's sake.

God's answer to that was as follows:

Amos 1:14 *But I will kindle a fire in the wall of Rabbah, and it shall devour the palaces thereof, with shouting in the day of battle, with a tempest in the day of the whirlwind:* **15** *And their king shall go into captivity, he and his princes together, saith the LORD.*

Rabbah was the capital city of the Ammonites. God determined to devour its palaces with shouting in the day of battle, and with tempest in the day of the whirlwind. These pictures describe chaos and pandemonium and utter destruction and a helplessness before it all.

Their king and their princes would all go into captivity.

Amos was not the only prophet to prophesy this. Jeremiah did as well, in dramatic detail:

Jeremiah 49:3 *Howl, O Heshbon, for Ai is spoiled: cry, ye daughters of Rabbah, gird you with sackcloth; lament, and run to and fro by the hedges; for their king shall go into captivity, and his priests and his princes together.*

If all of this makes it seem like a bad idea to line up against the Jews, that is because it is.

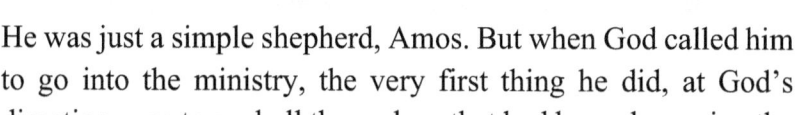

He was just a simple shepherd, Amos. But when God called him to go into the ministry, the very first thing he did, at God's direction, was to eyeball the wolves that had been devouring the sheep and start swinging the staff at all of them.

Good shepherd, that.

Chapter Six
Over The Target

Amos 2:1 *Thus saith the LORD; For three transgressions of Moab, and for four, I will not turn away the punishment thereof; because he burned the bones of the king of Edom into lime:* **2** *But I will send a fire upon Moab, and it shall devour the palaces of Kerioth: and Moab shall die with tumult, with shouting, and with the sound of the trumpet:* **3** *And I will cut off the judge from the midst thereof, and will slay all the princes thereof with him, saith the LORD.* **4** *Thus saith the LORD; For three transgressions of Judah, and for four, I will not turn away the punishment thereof; because they have despised the law of the LORD, and have not kept his commandments, and their lies caused them to err, after the which their fathers have walked:* **5** *But I will send a fire upon Judah, and it shall devour the palaces of Jerusalem.* **6** *Thus saith the LORD; For three transgressions of Israel, and for four, I will not turn away the punishment thereof; because they sold the righteous for silver, and the poor for a pair of shoes;* **7** *That pant after the dust of the earth on the head of the poor, and turn aside the way of the meek: and a man and his father will go in unto the same maid, to profane my holy name:* **8** *And they lay themselves down upon clothes laid to pledge by every altar, and they drink the wine of the condemned in the house of their god.* **9** *Yet destroyed I the Amorite before them, whose height was like* *the height of the cedars, and he was strong as the oaks; yet I destroyed his fruit from above, and his roots from beneath.* **10** *Also I brought you up from the land of Egypt, and led you forty years through the wilderness, to possess the land of the Amorite.* **11** *And I raised up of your sons for prophets, and of your young men for Nazarites. Is it not even thus, O ye children of Israel? saith the LORD.* **12** *But ye gave the Nazarites wine to drink; and commanded the prophets, saying, Prophesy not.* **13** *Behold, I am pressed under you, as a cart is pressed that is full of sheaves.* **14** *Therefore the flight shall perish from the swift, and the strong shall not strengthen his force, neither shall the mighty deliver himself:* **15** *Neither shall he stand that handleth the bow; and he that is swift of foot shall not deliver himself: neither shall he that rideth the horse deliver himself.* **16** *And he that is courageous among the mighty shall flee away naked in that day, saith the LORD.*

Amos spent all of chapter one swinging his shepherd's staff at the enemies of Israel. There is no doubt whatsoever that his entire message in that chapter received a hearty amen of approval from everyone in the Northern Kingdom.

But they were perhaps a bit wary as he began chapter two. Why would more message be needed with all the nations that he blistered in chapter one? If he wasn't careful, he may end up having some of his words of judgment land on the wrong people, say, them, for instance.

As it turns out, he was going to do just that.

But not as collateral damage.

They were actually the main target all along.

Judgment a block over

Amos 2:1 *Thus saith the LORD; For three transgressions of Moab, and for four, I will not turn away the* *punishment thereof; because he burned the bones of the king of Edom into lime:*

Just to the east of the Jordan River and the Dead Sea lay the territory of Moab. Moab was the second of the two sons born to the incestuous daughters of Lot, Ammon being the other. Amos was now very much getting into the neighborhood of Israel with his messages of judgment.

Interestingly, while all of the judgments in chapter one dealt with how other nations, including Edom, treated Israel, this judgment centers on how Moab treated Edom. In plain terms, this was bad guy versus bad guy, and yet, God was interested in how everything played out.

The account given to us here is given nowhere else in Scripture; we do not know where and when and how this happened. We do know that God was furiously angry over it. And what makes that all the more interesting is that this was not anger over someone who had been unjustly killed; this was anger over how a dead body was handled. God specifically castigated Moab for burning the bones of the king of Edom to powdered lime. In other words, this Edomite king, whoever he was, had been long since dead. This, then, was an insult, the desecration of a dead body just to prove a point.

Why in the world would such a thing draw the ire of God to that degree? Mostly because we are the only beings on the face of the earth made in His image. Therefore, whether in death or in life, anything that is done with the intent of desecrating that image is an insult to God, our Creator Himself.

Here is what God determined to do based on that final act of wickedness from a wicked people:

Amos 2:2 *But I will send a fire upon Moab, and it shall devour the palaces of Kerioth: and Moab shall die with tumult, with shouting, and with the sound of the trumpet:*

Kerioth was the chief city of Moab, the capital city, in our vernacular. In Isaiah 15:1 it was called Kir of Moab. God was going to send a fire, meaning the fires of war, to Moab. Those fires would destroy their capital city and all of the palaces therein. Moab as a kingdom was going to *die with tumult, with shouting, and with the sound of the trumpet.* These words tell in the most picturesque form of the chaos and pandemonium in Moab as they later fell to Babylon, along with most of the nations around them.

Jeremiah spoke of the same thing in equally picturesque words:

Jeremiah 48:41a *Kerioth is taken, and the strong holds are surprised...*

A result of this surprising fall was laid out in verse three:

Amos 2:3 *And I will cut off the judge from the midst thereof, and will slay all the princes thereof with him, saith the LORD.*

The government, the line of rulers, was going to be cut off. As with the Philistines, who are found no more after Zechariah 9:6, no mention of Moab is found after Zephaniah 2:9:

Zephaniah 2:9 *Therefore as I live, saith the LORD of hosts, the God of Israel, Surely Moab shall be as Sodom, and the children of Ammon as Gomorrah, even the breeding of nettles, and saltpits, and a perpetual desolation: the residue of my people shall spoil them, and the remnant of my people shall possess them.*

Moab has indeed died, being either exterminated or assimilated entirely.

Judgment at the neighbor's house

Amos 2:4 *Thus saith the LORD; For three transgressions of Judah, and for four, I will not turn away the punishment thereof; because they have despised the law of the*

LORD, and have not kept his commandments, and their lies caused them to err, after the which their fathers have walked:

In spite of their long enmity against their relatives, Judah, the people of Israel likely got a bit of a sick feeling in their stomachs when they heard or read these words from Amos. Though the two kingdoms may be separated, they all came from Abraham. If God was willing to bring the judgment next door to their family in Judah, they had to have an inkling by now that Judah might not be the last stop in God's tour of judgment.

God said that He was angry with Judah *because they have despised the law of the LORD, and have not kept his commandments, and their lies caused them to err, after the which their fathers have walked:*

One of the things that makes this description so interesting is that Amos was giving it during the reign of King Uzziah. Uzziah reigned for fifty-two years, starting from the age of sixteen, and most of them were good and godly and prosperous years. He was a successful builder, a successful battler, and one who elevated the kingdom to heights of prosperity and glory not seen since the days of Solomon.

Uzziah, though, made one crucial mistake in his older years:

2 Chronicles 26:16 *But when he was strong, his heart was lifted up to his destruction: for he transgressed against the LORD his God, and went into the temple of the LORD to burn incense upon the altar of incense.* **17** *And Azariah the priest went in after him, and with him fourscore priests of the LORD, that were valiant men:* **18** *And they withstood Uzziah the king, and said unto him, It appertaineth not unto thee, Uzziah, to burn incense unto the LORD, but to the priests the sons of Aaron, that are consecrated to burn incense: go out of the sanctuary; for thou hast trespassed; neither shall it be for thine honour from the LORD God.* **19** *Then Uzziah was wroth, and had a censer in* *his hand to burn incense: and while he was wroth with the priests, the leprosy even rose up in his forehead before the priests in the house of the LORD, from beside the incense altar.* **20** *And Azariah the chief priest, and all the priests, looked upon him, and, behold, he was leprous in his forehead, and they thrust him out from thence; yea, himself hasted also to go out, because the LORD had smitten him.* **21** *And Uzziah the king was a leper unto the day of his death, and dwelt in a several house, being a leper; for he was cut off from the house of the LORD: and Jotham his son was over the king's house, judging the people of the land.*

Uzziah intruded into the priesthood and was smitten with leprosy by God for that error. I point that out because the words of God in judgment against Israel clearly do not fit that one error of the then-ruling king. Here was the accusation again:

…They have despised the law of the LORD, and have not kept his commandments, and their lies caused them to err, after the which their fathers have walked:

Of note, here, are the usages of the plural pronouns "they" and "their." It was not the singular sin of Uzziah that caused God to come against them in judgment; it was the long-term disobedience of the people despising the law of the Lord, disobeying His commandments, and being liars instead of truth-tellers, all of which they learned from their fathers, meaning those who came before them. Yes, they had good kings sprinkled in among the bad, a luxury that the Northern Kingdom of Israel never had. But as a whole, the people and their rulers grew more and more wicked with each passing generation until God would no longer extend them a hand of mercy and chose instead to come against them in judgment.

And here is how He described that judgment:

Amos 2:5 *But I will send a fire upon Judah, and it shall devour the palaces of Jerusalem.*

Scripture does not merely give us the assurance of Amos's prophecy; it also gives us a detailed and vivid description of its fulfillment:

2 Kings 25:1 *And it came to pass in the ninth year of his reign, in the tenth month, in the tenth day of the month, that Nebuchadnezzar king of Babylon came, he, and all his host, against Jerusalem, and pitched against it; and they built forts against it round about.* **2** *And the city was besieged unto the eleventh year of king Zedekiah.* **3** *And on the ninth day of the fourth month the famine prevailed in the city, and there was no bread for the people of the land.* **4** *And the city was broken up, and all the men of war fled by night by the way of the gate between two walls, which is by the king's garden: (now the Chaldees were against the city round about:) and the king went the way toward the plain.* **5** *And the army of the Chaldees pursued after the king, and overtook him in the plains of Jericho: and all his army were scattered from him.* **6** *So they took the king, and brought him up to the king of Babylon to Riblah; and they gave judgment upon him.* **7** *And they slew the sons of Zedekiah before his eyes, and put out the eyes of Zedekiah, and bound him with fetters of brass, and carried him to Babylon.* **8** *And in the fifth month, on the seventh day of the month, which is the nineteenth year of king Nebuchadnezzar king of Babylon, came Nebuzaradan, captain of the guard, a servant of the king of Babylon, unto Jerusalem:* **9** *And he burnt the house of the LORD, and the king's house, and all the houses of Jerusalem, and every great man's house burnt he with fire.*

When God, through Amos, gave this prophecy of Judah's coming destruction, please understand that it was nowhere on the horizon. King Uzziah was actually pretty early in the history of the Southern Kingdom; there were at least eight more kings to come before Judah would finally fall. Only God could have accurately predicted such a thing and seen it come to be in such exacting detail.

Judgment in the living room

Amos 2:6a *Thus saith the LORD; For three transgressions of Israel, and for four, I will not turn away the punishment thereof...*

Amos has now arrived at the ultimate target for his prophecy—Israel. The ones who had cheered at the coming judgment against all of their hated adversaries, and even their estranged family, must now endure the focus being squarely on them. And while everyone else received a scant few verses concerning their disobedience and coming judgment, Israel was going to be the exclusive focus for seven and a half chapters or more.

Amos 2:6b *...because they sold the righteous for silver, and the poor for a pair of shoes;*

God's first accusation against His people of Israel was that they treated their own indebted countrymen as trinkets to be sold for a paltry price. Even the most righteous among them were regarded as nothing more than a way to gain a few silver coins. The poor brought less than that; rather than simply forgive their minuscule debts, they would be sold for the price of a pair of shoes. After all, the kids can't be re-wearing last year's sandals, now can they?

Amos 2:7 *That pant after the dust of the earth on the head of the poor, and turn aside the way of the meek: and a man and his father will go in unto the same maid, to profane my holy name:*

Three more accusations are now laid to Israel's charge. The first is that they *pant after the dust of the earth on the head of the poor*. This obscure-sounding phrase is designed to paint a ridiculous picture to show the almost beyond satire level of greed that the people had devolved to. It paints the picture of a person who is so poor that all he has, as he lays by the side of the road, is the very dust on his head. And yet people are so greedy that, when they see that layer of dust, they determine to take even that from him.

The second accusation given in verse seven is that they *turn aside the way of the meek.* In other words, when they see the meekest members of society simply going on their way, not harming a soul, they determine to somehow trip them up.

Verse seven's third accusation is the most lurid of all. God said *a man and his father will go in unto the same maid, to profane my holy name.*

Full-well aware of God's clear and strict commands for human sexuality, including all of the prohibitions of Leviticus 18 that were designed both to forbid sodomy and to produce clear lines of separation between family and any sexual activity, fathers and sons in Judah would seek out a woman that they could both go in unto. I trust that I do not need to explain how all of this was violated at the same time in the same moment by what Amos was describing. And all of it was intentional; they did it for the purpose of profaning the holy name of God by their unholiness.

Verse eight lays out yet more accusations:

Amos 2:8 *And they lay themselves down upon clothes laid to pledge by every altar, and they drink the wine of the condemned in the house of their god.*

The first of two accusations given in verse eight is that they *lay themselves down upon clothes laid to pledge by every altar.*

Here is what this sin was about:

Exodus 22:26 *If thou at all take thy neighbour's raiment to pledge, thou shalt deliver it unto him by that the sun goeth down:* **27** *For that is his covering only, it is his raiment for his* *skin: wherein shall he sleep? and it shall come to pass, when he crieth unto me, that I will hear; for I am gracious.*

If a person pledged his outer garment as collateral for a loan, the person to whom he gave it as collateral was required to give it back to him each and every day before the sun set so that he could sleep in it and not be cold. But Israel devolved to a state that not only were they not returning that needed outer garment of a poor debtor, but they were laying it on the altars of their idols and then sleeping on it so that the debtor could not get it from them. It was as if they were greedily hugging their emotional support teddy bear when what they were really doing was fully embracing their own greed in defiance of the compassionate law of God on the subject.

The second accusation given against them in verse eight is that *they drink the wine of the condemned in the house of their god.*

These words go back to the instructive words of the Proverbs:

Proverbs 31:6 *Give strong drink unto him that is ready to perish, and wine unto those that be of heavy hearts.*

What did Lemuel's mother mean when she told her son, the king, to give strong drink unto him that is ready to perish, and wine unto those that had heavy hearts?

Adam Clarke explains:

> "Inebriating drinks were mercifully given to condemned criminals, to render them less sensible of the torture they endured in dying. This is what was offered to our Lord; but he refused it." (Clarke, 3:792)

As a king, Lemuel was going to be in charge of meting out the death penalty. And whether we like it or not, in those days it was usually not a quick and painless affair. And so, to those who were dying, most specifically to those who were being put to death, and thus of a heavy heart, alcohol was a merciful thing. And yet, things got so bad in Israel that when a condemned man was on his way to a torturous death, they took that singular relief from him, brought it to the house of their gods, and boozed it up with it.

Why would Israel behave in such an unbelievably horrible and dirty manner? Mostly because they thought they were too special for God to ever judge them.

They were going to be sorely disappointed in how that worked out:

Amos 2:9 *Yet destroyed I the Amorite before them, whose height was like the height of the cedars, and he was strong as the oaks; yet I destroyed his fruit from above, and his roots from beneath.*

While Israel was away in their years of bondage in Egypt, the Amorites inhabited the land. God spoke to Abraham of this in Genesis 15:16, saying, *But in the fourth generation they shall come hither again: for the iniquity of the Amorites is not yet full.*

God, through Amos, reminded Israel that the Amorites, who had dwelt in that very same land that they now inhabited, were tall and strong like the cedars. The Amorites were the strongest of all the Canaanite nations and the ones that Israel most feared when they realized they had to face them. And yet, God drove them out. He wrecked them from top to bottom and poetically expresses that here in the words *yet I destroyed his fruit from above, and his roots from beneath.*

This verse is designed both as a reminder to Israel of God's mercies and as assurance that if the Amorites could not withstand His judgment, neither will they be able to do so.

Amos 2:10 *Also I brought you up from the land of Egypt, and led you forty years through the wilderness, to possess the land of the Amorite.*

Israel is now given a verse that is entirely a reminder of God's mercy and goodness. He is the one who brought them out of Egypt's bondage, led them and supplied them for forty years in the wilderness, and then brought them into the Promised Land and drove the feared Amorites out from before them.

Amos 2:11 *And I raised up of your sons for prophets, and of your young men for Nazarites. Is it not even thus, O ye children of Israel? saith the LORD.*

To Israel, this reminded instance of God's goodness may not have meant much. But to God, it was the most precious of all; this and this alone receives His exasperated cry, *Is it not even thus, O ye children of Israel?* God raised up some of their sons for prophets and their young men for Nazarites. He made their boys into men like Elijah and Elisha and Nathan and Gad and Isaiah and Daniel. God raised up others of their sons, men like Samson and Samuel, to be Nazarites, visibly separated to God and empowered by God.

But these gifts fell to men who had little to no regard for them. In fact, they regarded them as jokes to be had and irritations to be dealt with:

Amos 2:12 *But ye gave the Nazarites wine to drink; and commanded the prophets, saying, Prophesy not.*

One of the three significant vows of the Nazarite was that they were never to touch any fruit of the vine in any form. But rather than respecting that restraint and recognizing the purity and holiness it called an entire nation to, the people instead put alcohol in front of the Nazarites and tempted them to drink it until they gave in. The prophets were handled differently and more directly; they were repeatedly commanded to shut up and stop saying things that people did not like to hear.

Amos 2:13 *Behold, I am pressed under you, as a cart is pressed that is full of sheaves.*

It is God, not Amos, that is doing the speaking with this word picture that is given in verse thirteen. He pictures Himself as a cart that is so loaded down that the axles are about to break. And they themselves are the sheaves that He is loaded down with, the load that is about to make Him stop and dump everything and cast it aside.

Amos 2:14 *Therefore the flight shall perish from the swift, and the strong shall not strengthen his force, neither shall the mighty deliver himself:* **15** *Neither shall he stand that handleth the bow; and he that is swift of foot shall not deliver himself: neither shall he that rideth the horse deliver himself.*

Any nation with a strong military and mighty warriors is at risk; specifically, they are at risk of thinking that because of their military might, they cannot fall, no matter what God says to the contrary. But God uses these two verses to describe the different categories and avenues of the strength that was available to Israel and why none of them would avail in the day of judgment.

Flight shall perish from the swift: the speed that you have depended on will disappear from your very fastest runners.

The strong shall not strengthen his force: those who need their strength to increase will instead find it decreasing when they need it the most.

Neither shall the mighty deliver himself: your greatest warriors will not even be able to save themselves, let alone save you.

Neither shall he stand that handleth the bow: your bowman will not stay in place and shoot their arrows; they will flee away along with everyone else.

He that is swift of foot shall not deliver himself: your very fastest will not escape.

Neither shall he that rideth the horse deliver himself: even those fleeing away on horses will not be fast enough to escape.

And as one final indignity, chapter two ends this way:

Amos 2:16 *And he that is courageous among the mighty shall flee away naked in that day, saith the LORD.*

What horror that their mightiest warriors would, in Appalachian vernacular, "Get beat slam nekkid and run like scalded cats!"

And yet that is exactly what was going to happen.

But not to Damascus, Gaza, Tyre, Edom, Ammon, Moab, or Judah.

It was going to happen to Israel.

Chapter Seven
Jilted

Amos 3:1 *Hear this word that the LORD hath spoken against you, O children of Israel, against the whole family which I brought up from the land of Egypt, saying,* **2** *You only have I known of all the families of the earth: therefore I will punish you for all your iniquities.* **3** *Can two walk together, except they be agreed?* **4** *Will a lion roar in the forest, when he hath no prey? will a young lion cry out of his den, if he have taken nothing?* **5** *Can a bird fall in a snare upon the earth, where no gin is for him? shall one take up a snare from the earth, and have taken nothing at all?* **6** *Shall a trumpet be blown in the city, and the people not be afraid? shall there be evil in a city, and the LORD hath not done it?* **7** *Surely the Lord GOD will do nothing, but he revealeth his secret unto his servants the prophets.* **8** *The lion hath roared, who will not fear? the Lord GOD hath spoken, who can but prophesy?* **9** *Publish in the palaces at Ashdod, and in the palaces in the land of Egypt, and say, Assemble yourselves upon the mountains of Samaria, and behold the great tumults in the midst thereof, and the oppressed in the midst thereof.* **10** *For they know not to do right, saith the LORD, who store up violence and robbery in their palaces.* **11** *Therefore thus saith the Lord GOD; An adversary there shall be even round about the land; and he shall bring down thy strength from thee, and thy palaces shall be spoiled.* **12** *Thus saith the LORD; As the shepherd taketh* *out of the mouth of the lion two legs, or a piece of an ear; so shall the children of Israel be taken out that dwell in Samaria in the corner of a bed, and in Damascus in a couch.* **13** *Hear ye, and testify in the house of Jacob, saith the Lord GOD, the God of hosts,* **14** *That in the day that I shall visit the transgressions of Israel upon him I will also visit the altars of Bethel: and the horns of the altar shall be cut off, and fall to the ground.* **15** *And I will smite the winter house with the summer house; and the houses of ivory shall perish, and the great houses shall have an end, saith the LORD.*

In chapter two of the book of Amos, Israel realized that it was not just all of the nations around her that were to be a target of the prophecy of coming judgment from God; they were to be included as well. In fact, they were the main target the entire time.

In chapter three, Amos will begin to lay out God's case against His people.

A love spurned

Amos 3:1 *Hear this word that the LORD hath spoken against you, O children of Israel, against the whole family which I brought up from the land of Egypt, saying,* **2** *You only have I known of all the families of the earth: therefore I will punish you for all your iniquities.*

In the first couple of chapters of the book of Amos, there is a fairly simple and normal word that does not occur. I point that out at this point because it does appear here at the start of chapter three—and the start of chapter four and the start of chapter five. It is the word *hear*:

Amos 3:1 *Hear this word that the LORD hath spoken against you, O children of Israel*

Amos 4:1 *Hear this word, ye kine of Bashan, that are in the mountain of Samaria...*

Amos 5:1 _Hear ye this word which I take up against you, even a lamentation, O house of Israel._

God never had to tell the heathen to hear, to listen, in this prophecy of Amos. But in three straight chapters, He had to begin by telling His people, Israel, to hear, to listen, to pay attention. It is almost as if He knew them well enough to know that they were actually the least likely ones to be willing to pay attention to what He had to say, even though it should have been the exact opposite.

What is it exactly that He wanted them to hear? To begin with, He wanted them to hear a reminder that they were _the whole family which I brought up from the land of Egypt._ They were then to hear and remember that _You only have I known of all the families of the earth..._

As is quite often the case with the word _know_ in the Old Testament, this was not simply the awareness of a fact as we tend to take the word. This was a word of intimacy. It is from the word _yawdah,_ and is the same word used in Genesis 4:1, where we read, _And Adam knew Eve his wife; and she conceived._

This was God reminding Israel that He chose to know them in a more intimate and personal way than any other nation on Earth, just like a husband knows his wife in a more personal and intimate way than any other woman on Earth.

This was the highest of stations and the most precious of privileges. And it is on that basis that God shows His anger in the book of Amos. He says at the end of verse two, _therefore_ [because I have been so intimate with you and you have chosen to disobey me] _I will punish you for all your iniquities._

If God never made Himself known to people and never loved them and never cared for them, there would be much less of an observable basis for anger at iniquity. But when God has joined Himself in love to a person or people, He takes it very personally when they spurn that love in favor of iniquity.

A list of questions

Amos 3:3 *Can two walk together, except they be agreed?*

This verse is one of the better-known verses of Scripture, very often quoted, even if someone cannot tell you the exact reference. But what is not as well-known is its context and that it is a part of a series of questions, not merely an individual question unto itself. Between verses three and eight, you will find nine questions back-to-back, with one statement in between them in verse seven that helps to set the context:

Amos 3:7 *Surely the Lord GOD will do nothing, but he revealeth his secret unto his servants the prophets.*

The context of the famous question of verse three and all of the lesser-known questions that follow, then, is the fact that Amos and the rest of the prophets were speaking the words of God, not their own opinion. This series of questions was designed to remind people that they should pay attention to the words being spoken and they should hear, as verse one instructed them.

With that understanding, let's begin in verse three and work our way through these verses and these questions.

Amos 3:3 *Can two walk together, except they be agreed?*

I would estimate that ninety-nine times out of one hundred, when this verse is used, it is used as an admonition that we should not be walking in fellowship with those with whom we disagree about foundational issues of the faith or serious matters of morality/immorality. And the entire context of Scripture does back up that assertion. For instance:

2 Corinthians 6:17 *Wherefore come out from among them, and be ye separate, saith the Lord, and touch not the unclean thing; and I will receive you,* **18** *And will be a Father unto you, and ye shall be my sons and daughters, saith the Lord Almighty.*

Titus 3:10 *A man that is an heretick after the first and second admonition reject;* **11** *Knowing that he that is such is subverted, and sinneth, being condemned of himself.*

So, applying Amos 3:3 that way does indeed fit with the subject as seen throughout Scripture and does no violence to the text whatsoever. That said, there was a nearer issue at play when Amos spoke and wrote these words. The main point Amos was making when he spoke and wrote them was that he and God and the other truly sent prophets were walking together and that their prophecies should, therefore, not be disregarded by Israel. It all goes back to the command to hear; God spoke to Amos, Amos spoke to the people, God and Amos were walking together, so everyone needed to listen.

Amos 3:4 *Will a lion roar in the forest, when he hath no prey? will a young lion cry out of his den, if he have taken nothing?*

In the two questions of this verse and in the questions of the verses to come, cause and effect are in view.

The questions of verse four revolve around the roaring of a lion. A lion may make noises at most any time; but that which Scripture here classifies as a roar is something that it does primarily when it has the prey in sight with no hope of the prey escaping. Listen to Keil and Delitzsch quoting Bochart: "The most terrible feature in the roaring of a lion is that with this... it declares war. And after the roar there immediately follows both slaughter and laceration. For, as a rule, it only roars with that sharp roar when it has the prey in sight, upon which it immediately springs." (Keil, 1:260)

It is much the same with the young lion; they roar in a roar of triumph when they have slaughtered and eaten, not when they have failed and are hungry.

Amos is not just making a point from nature; when he gets to verse eight, he is going to point out that God is the lion that he is talking about through this picture. And when the lion that is roaring is God, and you yourself are the prey, bad things are about to happen.

Amos 3:5 *Can a bird fall in a snare upon the earth, where no gin* [baited lure] *is for him? shall one take up a snare from the earth, and have taken nothing at all?*

The expected answer to all the questions given thus far is no. And that applies to the questions we find here in verse five as well. A bird is not going to get trapped in a trap that does not exist, chasing bait that is not there. Nor is a person going to pick up a snare that does not have anything in it; he will leave it there until it does have something in it.

Once again, these questions both deal with cause and effect and also paint a picture of personages. Just as Hosea pictured Israel as a silly bird who would be caught in a snare, Amos is doing the same thing here. Their desire for sin became the bait that would lead to their deep subjugation.

Amos 3:6a *Shall a trumpet be blown in the city, and the people not be afraid?*

Once again, the expected answer to this question is no. When a trumpet, a sound of alarm, rang through the city, everyone was immediately afraid because they knew bad things were coming. This was still cause and effect, but also a reminder that the trumpet of alarm would be sounded in their cities and that they would need to be afraid.

Amos 3:6b *...shall there be evil in a city, and the LORD hath not done it?*

Although it may sound surprising to some, the answer to this question is also an expected 'no'. It would do us good, therefore, to define the word *evil* as used in this verse, lest we find ourselves enmeshed in heresy and thinking horrible things about God that we ought not to think.

Evil in this verse is from the little word *ra,* and it is a very broad word. In many cases, it means evil in the sense we normally use it, as a synonym for sin. That usage of it clearly does not fit here, considering that it is the utterly holy God being spoken of. But one of the other very common meanings of it, harm or damage, fits both the holy nature of God and the context of the passage. Simply put, great harm and damage tied to the sin of the people was coming to the city, and it would be the holy God that brought it.

Amos 3:7 *Surely the Lord GOD will do nothing, but he revealeth his secret unto his servants the prophets.*

As we enjoy all of the blessings of our modern day, one of the blessings we enjoy is that we have the completed canon of Scripture. I would wager to say that most people have a dozen or more Bibles in their homes and can reach out and grab one and read the words of God in the Word of God anytime they desire. But in the days of Amos, that was not the case. They had some Scripture, but nowhere near all of it. But what they did have in those days, because of that lack of completed Scripture, were prophets. And the God who loved His people did not send judgment upon them without giving them any warning of the coming judgment; He always told the prophets and told the prophets to tell the people.

These words in the midst of this series of questions were Amos's way of trying to help the people. They were his way of trying to get them to pay attention and to do what he said so that the judgment could perhaps be stayed.

Amos 3:8 *The lion hath roared, who will not fear? the Lord GOD hath spoken, who can but prophesy?*

There was rarely a time in Israel's history when they responded properly to the warning of impending judgment given by the prophets. Thus, Amos, like so many before and so many after him, had to remind them that God the Lion had roared, and that they were to fear, and that the prophets were speaking at His command, not of their own choice.

God could not be killed, but prophets often were, so this was an immensely needed reminder.

A looming judgment

Amos 3:9 *Publish in the palaces at Ashdod, and in the palaces in the land of Egypt, and say, Assemble yourselves upon the mountains of Samaria, and behold the great tumults in the midst thereof, and the oppressed in the midst thereof.*

Samaria, the capital city of Israel, was surrounded by mountains. God sent word to the Philistines down in Ashdod and to the Egyptians over in Egypt to come up to those mountains and to look down on Samaria and watch all of the disaster that was unfolding. For comparison's sake, that would be something like God calling to North Korea and China and Russia to come hover over America and watch as we implode from within. It would be utter humiliation. And for Israel, it was all the more humiliating because these were (in their thinking) uncircumcised, backward heathens being called to witness against them. These were the people that Israel looked down on, the people that they thought they were better than because they, Israel, came from Abraham and had the law and had a little operation when they were eight days old.

The idea that "those people" would be witnessing their ruin was absolutely galling to them.

Why did it have to be like that, this combination of ruin and shame? The next verse gives that answer:

Amos 3:10 *For they know not to do right, saith the LORD, who store up violence and robbery in their palaces.*

Jamieson, Fausset, and Brown give an excellent explanation of the first phrase of this verse, saying, "Their moral corruption blinds their power of discernment so that they cannot do right. [This is] not simple intellectual ignorance; the defect lay in the heart and will." (Jamieson, 2:537)

If I may put it in my terms, they knew; they just chose not to know.

Because of this decision not to know, they became people *who store up violence and robbery in their palaces.*

This is often taken to mean that they store up the plunder from violence and robbery in their palaces. But while that may have indeed been the case, that misses the point of the intentional ridiculousness that God paints here in this picture. We are intended to view the rulers of Israel as people who were touring their palace storehouses in wonder and admiration at all of the violence and robbery they had heaped up for themselves; they viewed those things like rational people would view gold or silver. They had become so vile and violent that gore was as pleasing as the gold they had gained, and destruction was as desired as the diamonds they had accumulated.

But that kind of putrid philosophy comes at a high price:

Amos 3:11 *Therefore thus saith the Lord GOD; An adversary there shall be even round about the land; and he shall bring down thy strength from thee, and thy palaces shall be spoiled.*

Therefore. Because Israel was so vile and violent, God was going to raise up an adversary against them that would bring their strength tumbling down and plunder their palaces.

Not many years later, it came to be, just as Amos prophesied:

2 Kings 17:5 *Then the king of Assyria came up throughout all the land, and went up to Samaria, and besieged it three years.* **6** *In the ninth year of Hoshea the king of Assyria took Samaria, and carried Israel away into Assyria, and placed them in Halah and in Habor by the river of Gozan, and in the cities of the Medes.*

How bad was it? Amos gave that answer before it ever happened:

Amos 3:12 *Thus saith the LORD; As the shepherd taketh out of the mouth of the lion two legs, or a piece of an ear; so shall the children of Israel be taken out that dwell in Samaria in the corner of a bed, and in Damascus in a couch.*

In these ominous words, Israel is pictured as a lamb that has been devoured by a lion. By the time the shepherd gets there, all that is left are a couple of legs or a tiny piece of an ear; everything else has been utterly devoured.

The location from which they would be taken is picturesque, instructive, and stark. The text says *so shall the children of Israel be taken out that dwell in Samaria in the corner of a bed, and in Damascus in a couch.*

The corner of the bed and a couch were both terms that spoke of luxury and prominence. These were the choicest places in the land, or, in New Testament terms, the highest seat at the feast. It would not just be the weak, unprotected commoners that felt the brunt of the judgment; it would go all the way to the lords of the land in all of their luxury.

Amos 3:13 *Hear ye, and testify in the house of Jacob, saith the Lord GOD, the God of hosts,* **14** *That in the day that I shall visit the transgressions of Israel upon him I will also visit the altars of Bethel: and the horns of the altar shall be cut off, and fall to the ground.*

For a second time in this chapter and book, God instructs the children of Israel to hear; they do not want to hear, but He is requiring them to do so. This command to hear and testify is often viewed as being spoken to Amos and the prophets—and it was, but not to them alone. This is best regarded as a command for the prophets to speak the words to the people and for those people who hear to speak them to everyone else. This is to be a universal proclamation to Israel, the house of Jacob, because the impending judgment required no less.

The way God labeled Himself in this message of judgment was threatening; He called Himself the God of hosts, meaning the God of armies.

There was a time when those words were a source of comfort for Israel:

2 Samuel 5:10 *And David went on, and grew great, and the LORD God of hosts was with him.*

By the days of Amos, though, that was the last thing anyone wanted to hear since they had chosen to be on the opposite side of the battle line from that very God and His armies.

The purpose for which the God of hosts was coming is spelled out in verse fourteen: *That in the day that I shall visit the transgressions of Israel upon him I will also visit the altars of Bethel: and the horns of the altar shall be cut off, and fall to the ground.*

God was coming for a visit—but not a pleasant one. He was coming specifically to *visit the transgressions of Israel upon him,* meaning to reckon the number and apply the payment. God was, as it were, marching that way with His ledger book, and there was naught but wickedness and woe within it.

When He came, it would not just be to Israel in general; He intended to make a specific stop at a specific place for a specific purpose as well. He said, *I will also visit the altars of Bethel: and the horns of the altar shall be cut off, and fall to the ground.*

When Jeroboam introduced golden calf worship to the Northern Kingdom, he built a great altar there in Bethel, an altar with horns on its corners, which became stained with the blood of their victims. The priests of that idolatrous worship then proceeded to build their own smaller versions of that altar in other locations throughout the land:

Hosea 8:11 *Because Ephraim hath made <u>many altars</u> to sin, altars shall be unto him to sin.*

2 Chronicles 34:5 *And he burnt the bones of the priests upon <u>their altars</u>, and cleansed Judah and Jerusalem.*

God promised that He was going to come and cut off the horns of the altar and let them fall to the ground. Horns in Bible days were a symbol of power; God was going to cut off that power and humiliate the false gods that caused so much trouble amongst His people.

Amos 3:15 *And I will smite the winter house with the summer house; and the houses of ivory shall perish, and the great houses shall have an end, saith the LORD.*

Four descriptions pointing to one thing are seen in this verse that closes out Amos's third chapter. God mentions the winter house, the summer house, houses of ivory, and great houses.

Winter houses and summer houses meant the same thing then that they mean today. If you know someone who has a winter house and a summer house, say, a house by the beach and a house in the mountains, then you are generally dealing with someone who is very wealthy and lives in luxury. Ivory houses painted the same picture. For a house to be adorned or decorated with ivory and have ivory vessels within it marked a person as being one of great wealth. Great houses referred to size and splendor and the wealth that it took to procure and upkeep them.

But now look at the verse again, and notice the negatives instead of the positives:

Amos 3:15 *And I will **smite** the winter house with the summer house; and the houses of ivory shall **perish**, and the great houses shall **have an end**, saith the LORD.*

God was going to utterly wreck those who had the most and were, therefore, the most protected. And if the devastation was going to reach them, it was going to reach absolutely everyone.

In the 1600s, a new English word was coined: the word "jilted." It was a shortened form of a girl's name, the name Gillian, from whence we get the name Jill. It was used as a descriptive term for a woman who teased a man with the hope that she would be true to him and then gleefully dashed those hopes.

But God knew what that felt like way before Gillian, Jill, and jilted because Israel was *forever* doing that very thing to Him.

And as it turned out, God was not okay with being jilted, especially not by the only people He ever knew as closely and intimately as Israel.

He is still not okay with any of us jilting Him today, nor should we ever be okay with doing so.

Chapter Eight
Prepare To Meet Thy God

Amos 4:1 *Hear this word, ye kine of Bashan, that are in the mountain of Samaria, which oppress the poor, which crush the needy, which say to their masters, Bring, and let us drink.* **2** *The Lord GOD hath sworn by his holiness, that, lo, the days shall come upon you, that he will take you away with hooks, and your posterity with fishhooks.* **3** *And ye shall go out at the breaches, every cow at that which is before her; and ye shall cast them into the palace, saith the LORD.* **4** *Come to Bethel, and transgress; at Gilgal multiply transgression; and bring your sacrifices every morning, and your tithes after three years:* **5** *And offer a sacrifice of thanksgiving with leaven, and proclaim and publish the free offerings: for this liketh you, O ye children of Israel, saith the Lord GOD.* **6** *And I also have given you cleanness of teeth in all your cities, and want of bread in all your places: yet have ye not returned unto me, saith the LORD.* **7** *And also I have withholden the rain from you, when there were yet three months to the harvest: and I caused it to rain upon one city, and caused it not to rain upon another city: one piece was rained upon, and the piece whereupon it rained not withered.* **8** *So two or three cities wandered unto one city, to drink water; but they were not satisfied: yet have ye not returned unto me, saith the LORD.* **9** *I have smitten you with blasting and mildew: when your gardens and your vineyards and your fig trees and* *your olive trees increased, the palmerworm devoured them: yet have ye not returned unto me, saith the LORD.* **10** *I have sent among you the pestilence after the manner of Egypt: your young men have I slain with the sword, and have taken away your horses; and I have made the stink of your camps to come up unto your nostrils: yet have ye not returned unto me, saith the LORD.* **11** *I have overthrown some of you, as God overthrew Sodom and Gomorrah, and ye were as a firebrand plucked out of the burning: yet have ye not returned unto me, saith the LORD.* **12** *Therefore thus will I do unto thee, O Israel: and because I will do this unto thee, prepare to meet thy God, O Israel.* **13** *For, lo, he that formeth the mountains, and createth the wind, and declareth unto man what is his thought, that maketh the morning darkness, and treadeth upon the high places of the earth, The LORD, The God of hosts, is his name.*

God spent all of Amos 3 explaining to the people why He was so very angry with them. In short, it centered around the fact that He had chosen them as His special covenant people and had a relationship with them that He did not have with any other nation on earth. In spite of that, they had jilted Him, resulting in His righteous anger against them.

But there was still more to the story. Their refusal to walk with Him and obey Him had turned them into more than just a moral mess—it had turned them into monsters. As such, God was going to have a meeting with them, and it was not going to be a pleasant meeting.

An oppressive people

Amos 4:1 *Hear this word, ye kine of Bashan, that are in the mountain of Samaria, which oppress the poor, which crush the needy, which say to their masters, Bring, and let us drink.*

As we begin to examine this chapter's address from Amos, we should be reminded of the fact that, by trade, Amos dealt primarily in livestock. That fact is very important at this point as we begin to look at his opening words and the way he addresses his audience.

He calls them *kine of Bashan*.

Those words are not exactly part of the standard American vocabulary of the twenty-first century. This, then, is what you need to know. Bashan was a well-watered and fertile part of the land on the eastern side of the Jordan River between Hermon and Gilead. Anything that grew there, from plants to animals, generally tended to get really big and full.

Kine is an old English word for cows.

The man literally just called his audience "a bunch of fat cows." And, adding fitting insult to needed injury, as we will see from the terms of authority he will shortly use, these were mostly men he was talking to, men that he would not even dignify with the term bulls, but instead used the feminine word for heifers.

Amos was apparently not familiar with the modern ministerial mantra, "Above all else, be nice." Instead, he was familiar with a somewhat older ministerial mantra:

Isaiah 58:1 *Cry aloud, spare not, lift up thy voice like a trumpet, and shew my people their transgression, and the house of Jacob their sins.*

Amos was definitely "sparing not" when he called his people fat cows, kine of Bashan. But he was not being a pastoral shock-jock like so many modern jerks in suits; he was operating under the inspiration of God and saying exactly what needed to be said. The rest of the verse will explain that very well.

Amos 4:1b *...which oppress the poor, which crush the needy, which say to their masters, Bring, and let us drink.*

Amos's people, who were so well off that he described them as fat cows, were not getting that well-off by their hard work and wise investing. They were in ruling positions and positions of power, oppressing the poor. They were crushing the needy, and they were going in league with the masters of the poor and saying, in so many words, "Take what you can take from those weak and sorry saps, and then we will go and have a great time with it at happy hour."

They were God's people, which means they should have been good and merciful people, but they were instead oppressive people to those who were too weak to fight back.

An overwhelming shadow

Amos 4:2 *The Lord GOD hath sworn by his holiness, that, lo, the days shall come upon you, that he will take you away with hooks, and your posterity with fishhooks.* **3** *And ye shall go out at the breaches, every cow at that which is before her; and ye shall cast them into the palace, saith the LORD.*

In the words of these two verses, God has Amos cast a large, dark shadow over His people. He uses both a direct statement and an obvious metaphor to tell them what is coming in the future and why. He begins, though, by giving the level of certainty and the basis for His decision. Those two things are found in the phrase *The Lord GOD hath sworn by his holiness*.

Sworn. God has *shawbah*, He has taken a binding oath that this is what will be. And it will be because He has sworn *by his holiness*. His holiness is both the reason for what He will do and the guarantee upon which His oath rests. When God swears by His holiness, please understand that there is no firmer ground upon which any of His oaths could ever rest. Holiness is not what He does; it is what He is. This is recognized even by the angels of Heaven who unceasingly hover above His throne, crying, "Holy! Holy! Holy!"

If the oath that followed, then, were a positive thing, Israel could have rejoiced and rested assured in it. Instead, due to their iniquity, it was the exact opposite of a positive thing. The oath was: *lo, the days shall come upon you, that he will take you away with hooks, and your posterity with fishhooks. And ye shall go out at the breaches, every cow at that which is before her; and ye shall cast them into the palace, saith the LORD.*

I mentioned a moment ago that God uses both a direct statement and an obvious metaphor in these words. The direct statement comes first: *he will take you away with hooks, and your posterity with fishhooks.* This was a very real thing, not a word picture. The Assyrians had long since figured out how to make it very easy to bring a large number of captives from one place to another without those captives trying to escape or giving any trouble. They simply put fish hooks on lines in their noses and led them by those lines and hooks. (Jamieson, 2:540) God Himself even referenced this and told Assyria that He was going to do that to them during the reign of Hezekiah:

2 Kings 19:28 *Because thy rage against me and thy tumult is come up into mine ears, therefore I will put my hook in thy nose, and my bridle in thy lips, and I will turn thee back by the way by which thou camest.*

But by the days of Amos, Israel had gotten so wicked that God determined to let the Assyrians march in and put those hooks in the noses of His people and lead them as helpless, trembling captives into Assyria's distant lands. And this would not just be to them, the present adult generation. God said that this would also happen to their posterity. It would be their descendants, and even their children, that primarily bore the brunt of this painful and humiliating march into captivity.

The obvious metaphor in verse three is: *And ye shall go out at the breaches, every cow at that which is before her; and ye shall cast them into the palace, saith the LORD.*

I refer to this as an obvious metaphor because it goes right back to Amos, two verses earlier, calling his people fat cows.

When Assyria got to Samaria and finally broke down the walls, the nobles, the fat cows in the palace, were going to run for their lives through the breaches made in the wall. When they did, they were going to cast them, their posterity, as mentioned one verse earlier, onto the floor of the palace. They were literally going to throw their own children to the ground and abandon them so they could more quickly run for their own lives to try to escape the Assyrians.

An offensive offering

Amos 4:4 *Come to Bethel, and transgress; at Gilgal multiply transgression; and bring your sacrifices every morning, and your tithes after three years:*

Picture, if you will, a preacher taking out a nationwide television ad in which he stood in front of the cameras and told everyone, "Come on over to Widget Church and sin along with us! In fact, we will have a special Super Sin Day, where we sin as much as possible right there in the church!"

Shocking, right? And yet, that is the essence of what God was saying in the words, *Come to Bethel, and transgress; at Gilgal multiply transgression*. Bethel means "The House of God," and once upon a time in Israel, that was a fitting name for it. Gilgal was where the sin of Israel was taken away after the forty years of wandering in the wilderness. And yet, God now references those formerly holy places and invites everyone to come for a Sin Spectacular.

And if you sense a dramatic dose of Divine sarcasm in His words, then you get the point that others often miss here. It gets even more sarcastic when He adds, *and bring your sacrifices every morning, and your tithes after three years.* In other words, "Come on over to My house for a Super Sin Day, and as long as you drop your tithe into the plate, I, the God who needs nothing, will be perfectly satisfied with everything I see."

He is not done yet; the divine sarcasm continues into verse five:

Amos 4:5 *And offer a sacrifice of thanksgiving with leaven, and proclaim and publish the free offerings...*

So now we have something like "Come on over to My house for a Super Sin Day, and as long as you drop your tithe into the plate, I, the God who needs nothing, will be perfectly satisfied with everything I see, *especially* if you also add a little extra offering, and advertise it so that all of the other sinners can participate!"

And in case you are still not quite sure about the sarcasm angle, look at the last phrase of verse five:

...for this liketh you, O ye children of Israel, saith the Lord GOD.

So now you have something like, "Come on over to My house for a Super Sin Day, and as long as you drop your tithe into the plate, I, the God who needs nothing, will be perfectly satisfied with everything I see, *especially* if you also add a little extra offering, and advertise it so that all of the other sinners can participate, because you really like that, don't you, Israel?"

Do you understand what God is saying that makes Him so angry? His people are going to the House of God and wallowing around like a bunch of drunken alley cats, but they are perfectly satisfied with all of that because they have dropped a few pennies in the plate to tip God and "keep Him as happy as they are" with all of this mess.

They thought that their offerings bought them a pass on their iniquity, and that is the very definition of an offensive offering.

An ominous meeting

Amos 4:6 *And I also have given you cleanness of teeth in all your cities, and want of bread in all your places: yet have ye not returned unto me, saith the LORD.*

God had now sworn by His holiness that He was going to send the people into captivity in Assyria. And yet, this final judgment had not come without precursors, points at which they could have repented and avoided it. In this verse and the verses to follow, God will list some of the things He has already done with the intent of getting them to repent and be restored—things that they completely ignored and pushed past to their detriment.

Famine was first on the list. He said, *I also have given you cleanness of teeth in all your cities, and want of bread in all your places*. There was no need for dentists or dental hygienists in the days referenced by this phrase, simply because people had no food to eat by which they could dirty their teeth. One of the primary examples of this was the seven-year famine God sent in 2 Kings 8:1 during the days of Elisha.

You would think that seven years of famine and starvation would be enough to convince the people to return to God. Sadly, though, the verse ends with the words, *yet have ye not returned unto me, saith the LORD.*

He is going to use that accusatory phrase five times in this one short chapter.

Amos 4:7 *And also I have withholden the rain from you, when there were yet three months to the harvest: and I caused it to rain upon one city, and caused it not to rain upon another city: one piece was rained upon, and the piece whereupon it rained not withered.* **8** *So two or three cities wandered unto one city, to drink water; but they were not satisfied: yet have ye not returned unto me, saith the LORD.*

Drought was next on the list of precursor judgments. God allowed the rain pattern in Israel to become so sporadic and unpredictable that one city would experience a devastating drought while the city next to it had rain. People could not put down roots; they were having to move from city to city in search of water, and even when they got there, there was not enough water to go around.

But once again, we find the sad words, *yet have ye not returned unto me, saith the LORD.*

Amos 4:9 *I have smitten you with blasting and mildew: when your gardens and your vineyards and your fig trees and your olive trees increased, the palmerworm devoured them: yet have ye not returned unto me, saith the LORD.*

Blight on the crops was next on the list of precursor judgments. The food supply was attacked by blasting, which means blight, and by mildew, and by palmer worms, which is another word for locusts. All of this was timed in such a way that just when it seemed that a good, saving crop was coming in, the disaster would strike it.

But the stubbornness of the people held firm, and we once again see God saying, *yet have ye not returned unto me, saith the LORD.*

Amos 4:10 *I have sent among you the pestilence after the manner of Egypt: your young men have I slain with the sword, and have taken away your horses; and I have made the stink of your camps to come up unto your nostrils: yet have ye not returned unto me, saith the LORD.*

Pestilence was next on the list of precursor judgments, and after the manner of Egypt. In other words, God sent a series of judgments against His people that resembled the judgments He sent against Egypt to deliver His people from bondage so many years earlier. Bodies were stacked in the street to such a degree that everyone in the nation could smell the stench. How shocking, then, that we should once again find the words, *yet have ye not returned unto me, saith the LORD.*

Amos 4:11 *I have overthrown some of you, as God overthrew Sodom and Gomorrah, and ye were as a firebrand plucked out of the burning: yet have ye not returned unto me, saith the LORD.*

Fiery destruction was next in the list of precursor judgments. Adam Clarke paraphrased this well, saying, "In the destruction of your cities I have shown my judgments as signally as I did in the destruction of Sodom and Gomorrah; and those of you that did escape were as 'brands plucked out of the fire;' if not consumed, yet much scorched." (Clarke, 4:679)

Would all of that finally be enough? No. For the next thing we see yet again is: *yet have ye not returned unto me, saith the LORD.*

The problem with refusing to return to God and refusing to return to God and refusing to return to God is that you eventually reach the place of a *therefore*:

Amos 4:12 *Therefore thus will I do unto thee, O Israel: and because I will do this unto thee, prepare to meet thy God, O Israel.*

Therefore, because I sent you precursor judgment after precursor judgment and you would not repent and you would not return, *thus will I do unto thee, O Israel: and because I will do this unto thee, prepare to meet thy God, O Israel.*

Thus will I do unto thee refers back to God's promise to send the Assyrians to destroy their cities and drag them away with fish hooks. The worst part of that, though, was that that was not the worst part! The worst part was not going to be them meeting up with the Assyrians; the worst part was that their meeting with the Assyrians was going to send them to a meeting with God—a meeting that they were nowhere near prepared for.

They could have met Him in mercy and restoration; through their actions, they chose instead to meet Him as an adversary, an eternal mistake that could never be undone for any individual that made it.

Amos 4:13 *For, lo, he that formeth the mountains, and createth the wind, and declareth unto man what is his thought, that maketh the morning darkness, and treadeth upon the high places of the earth, The LORD, The God of hosts, is his name.*

Chapter four of the book of Amos ends in the most paradoxical of ways. The actual words of this verse could either be entirely comforting or wholly terrifying just as they are. In another context, set in one of the Psalms, for instance, these words could be words to cause national rejoicing in Israel or individual rejoicing from any child of God. But set as they are in this context of a rebellious and unrepentant people, these are instead some of the most terrifying words anyone could ever read.

In the first portion, God describes Himself in terms of omnipotence and omniscience in the words: *he that formeth the mountains, and createth the wind, and declareth unto man what is his thought, that maketh the morning darkness, and treadeth upon the high places of the earth.*

In the second portion, He designates Himself by name, saying, *The LORD, The God of hosts, is his name.* These words are God calling Himself Jehovah and Elohim Tsaba, the self-existing God, and the God of armies. To put it mildly, since the people had turned God into an adversary by turning themselves into the adversaries of God, these were the last descriptions of God or the last names of God that they would ever want to hear at that moment.

Prepare to meet thy God. When those words are spoken to a sinner who has the time and the capacity to repent, they are both warning words and wonderful words. But spoken as they were to people who had pushed beyond God's last measure of mercy, no more frightening words could ever have come from the lips of the prophet.

Be very careful about crossing God's deadlines, because He does have them.

Chapter Nine
What Are You Looking For?

Amos 5:1 *Hear ye this word which I take up against you, even a lamentation, O house of Israel.* **2** *The virgin of Israel is fallen; she shall no more rise: she is forsaken upon her land; there is none to raise her up.* **3** *For thus saith the Lord GOD; The city that went out by a thousand shall leave an hundred, and that which went forth by an hundred shall leave ten, to the house of Israel.* **4** *For thus saith the LORD unto the house of Israel,* **Seek** *ye me, and ye shall live:* **5** *But* **seek not** *Bethel, nor enter into Gilgal, and pass not to Beersheba: for Gilgal shall surely go into captivity, and Bethel shall come to nought.* **6 Seek** *the LORD, and ye shall live; lest he break out like fire in the house of Joseph, and devour it, and there be none to quench it in Bethel.* **7** *Ye who turn judgment to wormwood, and leave off righteousness in the earth,* **8 Seek** *him that maketh the seven stars and Orion, and turneth the shadow of death into the morning, and maketh the day dark with night: that calleth for the waters of the sea, and poureth them out upon the face of the earth: The LORD is his name:* **9** *That strengtheneth the spoiled against the strong, so that the spoiled shall come against the fortress.* **10** *They hate him that rebuketh in the gate, and they abhor him that speaketh uprightly.* **11** *Forasmuch therefore as your treading is upon the poor, and ye take from him burdens of wheat: ye have built houses of hewn stone, but ye shall not dwell* *in them; ye have planted pleasant vineyards, but ye shall not drink wine of them.* **12** *For I know your manifold transgressions and your mighty sins: they afflict the just, they take a bribe, and they turn aside the poor in the gate from their right.* **13** *Therefore the prudent shall keep silence in that time; for it is an evil time.* **14 Seek** *good, and not evil, that ye may live: and so the LORD, the God of hosts, shall be with you, as ye have spoken.*

Throughout Amos 4, God drove home the fact that since Israel had refused to return to Him, in spite of all the judgments He had sent, they were now to prepare to meet their God. This was not going to be a pleasant meeting; God was very much fed up with their wicked ways.

In this section of verses, God is going to deal with them about what they are seeking and about what they should be seeking.

A funeral song and its explanation

Amos 5:1 *Hear ye this word which I take up against you, even a lamentation, O house of Israel.*

Lamentation (25) or Lamentations (3) is found twenty-eight times in the Bible. You likely are aware of the fact that an entire book of the Bible is actually named Lamentations. We get our word lament from it, and it indicates a state of great sadness.

But there is much more to it than that. A lamentation was not just something that was sorrowfully said; in Bible terms, a lamentation was a dirge, an elegy, what we would call a funeral song. So, when the prophet Amos told Israel to listen very carefully as he sang their funeral song, believe me, people's jaws were dropping.

Israel had been having a few hard times of late, but this was still a very prosperous and powerful time in the kingdom. Any notion that the kingdom was about to die seemed far-fetched to the point of being fanatical. And yet, here was the prophet of God warming up his voice and perhaps an instrument and preparing to sing everyone the funeral dirge that God had given him for the nation.

That song, in its entirety, took one verse:

Amos 5:2 *The virgin of Israel is fallen; she shall no more rise: she is forsaken upon her land; there is none to raise her up.*

Think of Amos, with a silent and horrified crowd gathered around him, lifting his voice in a minor key and singing these words...

Why sing them? Why put this in the style of a funeral song? Why not just say them? Because nothing is as powerful and as easy to remember as music, especially music that breaks hearts. God wanted everyone in the land to take that short song back home with them and sing it to everyone who had not been there that day. He wanted it to spread so fast and so universally that from city to city and town to town and hillside to hillside, everyone's voices would join together in this mournful melody.

Here, again, was the content of that funeral song:

Amos 5:2 *The virgin of Israel is fallen; she shall no more rise: she is forsaken upon her land; there is none to raise her up.*

Whenever God spoke of Israel as a virgin, it was a very obvious euphemism for being unconquered. But now, with her still in her land and her king still on the throne, she is referred to as fallen; the fall is so certain that it is phrased as if it has already happened. Further, this fall is permanent; *she shall no more rise.*

When we read that *she is forsaken upon her land*, those words tie into what came immediately before them to complete the picture. Israel is shown as having fallen, and her fall is right there in her own land. And yet, she lies there utterly forsaken in the place where there should be the most help available to her; *there is none to raise her up.* This was the complete dissolution and dispersion of the ten tribes being spoken of; it was the death of the nation.

No wonder it was put in the form of a funeral song.

Amos 5:3 *For thus saith the Lord GOD; The city that went out by a thousand shall leave an hundred, and that which went forth by an hundred shall leave ten, to the house of Israel.*

This verse is the explanation of the funeral dirge that God gave Amos for the people. In short, ninety percent of them were going to be destroyed in the siege of Samaria by Shalmaneser; there would be a mere tenth to be carried away, a ravaged, defeated, ripped-up remnant. Bits and pieces would manage to make their way back to the land through the years, but the ten-tribe, Northern Kingdom of Israel, was forever dead.

A focused seeking and its effects

Amos 5:4 *For thus saith the LORD unto the house of Israel, Seek ye me, and ye shall live:*

In light of what we have just read and discussed, these words seem to present a bit of a riddle, don't they? Is the destruction of Israel a guaranteed thing or not? Is their fall and death really as certain as Amos just portrayed it, or is there still hope for them to be saved after all? Put another way, the first few verses assured them that they were going to die, and yet this verse and the following verses seem to assure them that there is the possibility for them to live, so which one of those two things is correct?

The answer is both—and also just the first one.

The key to all of that is this amazing thing called the foreknowledge of God: the fact that while He does not *cause* all things to happen, He does *know* all things that will happen.

In verses four through fourteen of this chapter, God is legitimately offering Israel a choice, a choice that will lead to them surviving and thriving. They absolutely have the opportunity to avert the death of the nation if they will just do what God says. But in verses one through three of this chapter, we see that God knows that they absolutely will not avail themselves of that opportunity, and thus, He pronounces them already dead.

In so many ways, this mirrors the foreknowledge of God in salvation. God offers salvation to all and yet knows from before the beginning the choice that every individual will make in that matter. He then pronounces them elect or non-elect based on that foreknowledge, all the while still offering a true choice and opportunity for *everyone* to be saved.

God's command to Israel here: *Seek ye me, and ye shall live,* also lets us know that mankind has both the ability and the responsibility to seek after God; God is not going to command people to do something that they cannot do and then punish them for what they could not do. This, though, also brings up another question we need to address:

Romans 3:11 *There is none that understandeth, there is none that seeketh after God.*

This verse is generally used by those of the Calvinist persuasion to claim that mankind cannot seek after God and that salvation is, therefore, simply a matter of Him arbitrarily choosing whom He will. And yet, God commands people to seek Him throughout the Scripture; we will see five instances of that in just this one chapter alone.

Romans 3:11 is a partial quote of Psalm 14:1-3:

Psalm 14:1 <To the chief Musician, A Psalm of David.> *The fool hath said in his heart, There is no God. They are corrupt, they have done abominable works, there is none that doeth good.* **2** *The LORD looked down from heaven upon the children of men, to see if there were any that did understand, and seek God.* **3** *They are all gone aside, they are all together become filthy: there is none that doeth good, no, not one.*

Note that in neither case does God say that no one *can* seek after Him; in both cases, He simply indicates that no one *is* seeking after Him. And yet, the Psalmist also said in Psalm 119:10, "*With my whole heart have I sought thee: O let me not wander from thy commandments.*" So clearly, we can seek after God, and some do.

In a nutshell, the reconciliation of all of this is that by ourselves, in our sinful flesh, we never could or would seek after God. But since God *draws all men to Himself* (John 12:32), everyone can and must respond to that drawing by seeking for God. Further, to take one or two verses that speak of man not seeking after God as an excuse to ignore the hundreds of verses and commands that we must seek after God is ministerial malpractice, to say the least.

God really meant it when He told Israel to seek after Him; He always means it when He tells anyone and everyone to seek after Him.

Amos 5:5 *But seek not Bethel, nor enter into Gilgal, and pass not to Beersheba: for Gilgal shall surely go into captivity, and Bethel shall come to nought.*

God, through Amos, clearly told the people to seek after Him and live. And yet, in His omniscience, He knew that while they may be listening, in their minds, they were already forming other plans. Specifically, He knew that there were three different *places* running through their minds that they intended to seek rather than seeking Him. Those places were Bethel and Gilgal and Beersheba.

These three places that they intended to seek had become three of the most ironic locations in the entire land. In their early years as a people, these were three of the holiest and most sacred places they could have ever come to visit, places where they could rightly have expected to have a meeting with God.

Bethel was the place where Jacob met with God and God spoke to him, a place that Jacob quickly recognized as the House of God, which the name itself signifies. Gilgal is the place where

God spoke to Joshua and rolled the reproach of Egypt off of Israel after forty years of wandering in the wilderness. Beersheba is the place where God spoke to Isaac.

And yet, by Amos's day, those three places had long since become centers of idolatry in Israel. Jeroboam's golden calf was in Bethel. Gilgal was the place of idols and pagan carvings where people came to worship. Beersheba was a place where the Israelites traveled to in idolatrous pilgrimages.

So, God told the people: *seek not Bethel, nor enter into Gilgal, and pass not to Beersheba: for Gilgal shall surely go into captivity, and Bethel shall come to nought.* These places that they intended to seek after instead of seeking after God, all of them, though He only gives details of the fall of two, were going to fall, just like all of the other places in the land. Their idols were going to be carried away into captivity.

Amos 5:6 *Seek the LORD, and ye shall live; lest he break out like fire in the house of Joseph, and devour it, and there be none to quench it in Bethel.*

This is now the second time in this chapter that God, through Amos, told the people that if they would seek Him, they would live. He phrased it as a promise here: *seek the Lord, and ye shall live.* But then He gave the "or else," saying, *lest he break out like fire in the house of Joseph, and devour it, and there be none to quench it in Bethel.*

When He speaks of the house of Joseph, it is a reference to the fact that Joseph's two children, Manasseh and Ephraim, were two of the biggest tribes of the Northern Kingdom of Israel. Thus, the house of Joseph is used here as another name for Israel. God was telling the people that if they did not seek after Him, He would break out like a fire in Israel and devour it, and there would be no one to put the fire out, not even Bethel, the erstwhile house of God.

Amos 5:7 *Ye who turn judgment to wormwood, and leave off righteousness in the earth,* **8** *Seek him that maketh the seven stars and Orion, and turneth the shadow of death into the morning, and maketh the day dark with night: that calleth for the waters of the sea, and poureth them out upon the face of the earth: The LORD is his name:* **9** *That strengtheneth the spoiled against the strong, so that the spoiled shall come against the fortress.*

These three verses make one long sentence. They begin in verse seven with God using a unique phrase of description against His people, calling them *Ye who turn judgment to wormwood, and leave off righteousness in the earth.*

There are nine different references to wormwood in the Scripture, the most famous of which is in the Book of The Revelation in the setting of the Tribulation Period:

Revelation 8:11 *And the name of the star is called Wormwood: and the third part of the waters became wormwood; and many men died of the waters, because they were made bitter.*

Those nine references refer to several different things. In the Book of The Revelation, the Greek word is *apsinthos,* and it refers to absinthe, a bitter yet highly addictive compound that has strong psychedelic and hallucinogenic effects and is also highly poisonous and often deadly. Through the years, it has often been used in different alcoholic drinks. In the Old Testament, it is from the Hebrew word *la-anah,* and it refers to a bitter plant. The next chapter in Amos will use the word *la-anah* again and name that plant for us:

Amos 6:12 *Shall horses run upon the rock? will one plow there with oxen? for ye have turned judgment into gall, and the fruit of righteousness into* **hemlock** [la-anah]:

Old Testament wormwood is hemlock. It is a bitter, deadly, poisonous plant; every single part of it can kill you. It used to be native mostly to the Mediterranean area of the world, but it is taking over many areas of the United States in our day and killing a lot of livestock along the way.

Its most famous victim was Socrates in 399 B.C.

With all of this understood, when God accused Israel of turning judgment to wormwood, He was accusing them of turning that which should have been beneficial, the judicial system, into something utterly bitter. This was a very common accusation that He leveled against them; they became notorious in the latter years of the kingdom for perverting judgment, taking bribes, and running roughshod over people who had no influence or means with which to defend themselves.

The last half of verse seven restates that accusation in different words, saying that they *leave off righteousness in the earth*. *Leave off* is from the word *yawnahk*, and it paints the picture of putting someone down for a long rest. It is as if proper judgment and righteousness were trying to make a change, and they were singing it to sleep so that it could not do so.

In verse eight, these people who had turned judgment to wormwood and sung righteousness to sleep were commanded to: *Seek him that maketh the seven stars and Orion, and turneth the shadow of death into the morning, and maketh the day dark with night: that calleth for the waters of the sea, and poureth them out upon the face of the earth: The LORD is his name:*

Had they sought their idols? Yes. Had it helped? No. But why? Well, partly because their idols were dumb hunks of wood that had never created a single thing and were themselves created by others. If Israel wanted a change that could stave off disaster, they were going to need to start seeking higher, much higher. In fact, they would need to start seeking after the God Who made the gigantic and magnificent things in the sky over their heads each night, things like the seven stars and Orion. The seven stars referred to Pleiades. Both Orion and Pleiades were mentioned in the book of Job, and Amos seems to be quoting from those passages, Job 9:9 and 38:31.

Further, the God that they were to be seeking was the God who *turneth the shadow of death into the morning* [makes the darkest night flee with the sunrise], *and maketh the day dark with night* [makes the sun set so the night can have its time]. He is the God *that calleth for the waters of the sea, and poureth them out upon the face of the earth* [sends the rains down either in judgment or in mercy]. And in case they still did not know who that God was and is, he said, *The LORD* [Jehovah] *is his name.*

That God, Jehovah, Amos then describes this way in verse nine: *That strengtheneth the spoiled against the strong, so that the spoiled shall come against the fortress.* Remember that one of the chief accusations God has been leveling against them is that they pervert judgment and oppress the poor. They had created a victim class, a mass of people who had no means or power to defend themselves. But God specifically chooses to be a God that strengthens people in pitiful conditions like that, and to such a degree that they will have the power even to march against the forces of evil that have trodden them down.

Amos 5:10 *They hate him that rebuketh in the gate, and they abhor him that speaketh uprightly.*

Things change in a dramatic way in verse ten. Amos has been speaking of the twisted and biased judicial system that the power brokers had put in place. And it seems that as he spoke these words to those powerful people, he was getting pushback, perhaps even threats, because he addressed others while pointing at them. He says to those who will listen, *They,* those powerful people, *they hate him that rebuketh in the gate.* They hate honest judges who will call them down and rule fairly. Further, *they abhor him that speaketh uprightly.*

That seems very much to have been directed at how they were responding to him, Amos the prophet; he was the one speaking uprightly, and they hated his guts for it. Amos publicly pointed this out. And he was going to continue directly addressing them in the next few verses:

Amos 5:11 *Forasmuch therefore as your treading is upon the poor, and ye take from him burdens of wheat: ye have built houses of hewn stone, but ye shall not dwell in them; ye have planted pleasant vineyards, but ye shall not drink wine of them.*

Amos accused the powerful men of his nation of treading on the poor, making them a profitable pathway under their feet. He accused them of taking *burdens of wheat* from the poor, meaning great portions of their wheat for taxes, tribute, or just because.

Through means of all of that dishonest gain, they had *built houses of hewn stone*. That kind of construction was extremely elaborate and expensive in those days; it still is, even in ours. But because of how they had gotten their houses and lands, God, through Amos, said, *but ye shall not dwell in them; ye have planted pleasant vineyards, but ye shall not drink wine of them*. When the Assyrians came in, they would all be carried away, and those fancy houses and lovely vineyards would fade into the distance as their owners were marched into a foreign land.

Amos 5:12 *For I know your manifold transgressions and your mighty sins: they afflict the just, they take a bribe, and they turn aside the poor in the gate from their right.*

God said that He knew their *manifold transgressions and mighty sins*; their sins were many, and they were powerful in their awful effect. Specifically, He said that *they afflict the just* [they punish the righteous], *they take a bribe* [right or wrong was determined by who could slide them the most money under the table], *and they turn aside the poor in the gate from their right* [they would not allow the poor to even have their case heard since they had nothing to bribe them with].

Clearly, things were very, very bad in Israel. So much so that Amos had to give the following guidance:

Amos 5:13 *Therefore the prudent shall keep silence in that time; for it is an evil time.*

When the justice system has become a pay-for-play scheme, the tendency is to stand up and shout against it and complain that it is unfair. And it is, but what good does it do to complain when that is the situation? Amos points out that all they would do is draw attention to themselves and that it would not end well, so the wiser course of action would be to simply shut up and never say anything about it.

That is the peak definition of *an evil time*.

Amos 5:14 *Seek good, and not evil, that ye may live: and so the LORD, the God of hosts, shall be with you, as ye have spoken.*

This verse presents the most bewildering thing to behold. In spite of all of the abject wickedness that had just been described, the people were confident they would never fall; they were confident of that because, in their words, "The LORD is with us." That is what Amos said that they had been saying. The prophet Micah pointed to that same senseless thing and in the same wicked setting:

Micah 3:11 *The heads thereof judge for reward, and the priests thereof teach for hire, and the prophets thereof divine for money: yet will they lean upon the LORD, and say, Is not the LORD among us? none evil can come upon us.*

They believed it. They really believed it. They were running roughshod over everyone and everything, worshipping their idols, and yet they believed that no evil could come upon them because "the LORD was among them." So Amos said,

Seek good, and not evil, that ye may live: and so the LORD, the God of hosts, shall be with you, as ye have spoken.

In other words, "Do you really want God to be among you? Do you really want to live and not die? The only way that is going to happen is if you start seeking good and not evil. As long as you are waking up every day and pursuing your sin and running over people in the process, God will not be among you, and you are not going to live. Until you start repenting and forsaking your sin and truly seeking after the God of righteousness, you are all doomed."

As it turns out, what you seek for determines what you end up finding. So, what are you looking for?

Chapter Ten
Be Careful What You Ask For

Amos 5:15 *Hate the evil, and love the good, and establish judgment in the gate: it may be that the LORD God of hosts will be gracious unto the remnant of Joseph.* **16** *Therefore the LORD, the God of hosts, the Lord, saith thus; Wailing shall be in all streets; and they shall say in all the highways, Alas! alas! and they shall call the husbandman to mourning, and such as are skilful of lamentation to wailing.* **17** *And in all vineyards shall be wailing: for I will pass through thee, saith the LORD.* **18** *Woe unto you that desire the day of the LORD! to what end is it for you? the day of the LORD is darkness, and not light.* **19** *As if a man did flee from a lion, and a bear met him; or went into the house, and leaned his hand on the wall, and a serpent bit him.* **20** *Shall not the day of the LORD be darkness, and not light? even very dark, and no brightness in it?* **21** *I hate, I despise your feast days, and I will not smell in your solemn assemblies.* **22** *Though ye offer me burnt offerings and your meat offerings, I will not accept them: neither will I regard the peace offerings of your fat beasts.* **23** *Take thou away from me the noise of thy songs; for I will not hear the melody of thy viols.* **24** *But let judgment run down as waters, and righteousness as a mighty stream.* **25** *Have ye offered unto me sacrifices and offerings in the wilderness forty years, O house of Israel?* **26** *But ye have borne the tabernacle of your Moloch and Chiun your images,* *the star of your god, which ye made to yourselves.* **27** *Therefore will I cause you to go into captivity beyond Damascus, saith the LORD, whose name is The God of hosts.*

In the first fourteen verses of Amos 5, Amos used the word *seek* five times. God was insistent that His people seek the right things and stop seeking the wrong things.

He expressed much the same sentiment in the last half of Amos 5, as he says in so many words, "Be careful what you ask for."

A tragic decision

Amos 5:15 *Hate the evil, and love the good, and establish judgment in the gate: it may be that the LORD God of hosts will be gracious unto the remnant of Joseph.*

In the writings of the prophets, sometimes the prophets will be quoting the words of the LORD, and other times they will be, under the inspiration of the Holy Ghost, commenting on the words of the LORD. This verse is Amos commenting on what God has said in the verses prior to it. We know this because he uses the words *it may be that the LORD God of hosts will be gracious unto the remnant of Joseph.*

He begins verse fifteen with an instruction for everyone to *Hate the evil, and love the good, and establish judgment in the gate*. This ties into what he has been accusing them of for the entire chapter, namely twisting the justice system into a pay-for-play scheme that ran roughshod over the poor and did not care about little things like right and wrong.

Amos's instructions were for them to do the most obvious thing in their judicial dealings: hate the evil, love the good, and establish the gate, the place where matters were heard, as a place of judgment rather than a place of favoritism and bribery. Would it stay God's hand of judgment? No, that was already certain. But what it may well do, Amos said, was result in God being merciful to the remnant of Joseph, meaning to what would be left of the ten tribes once the kingdom had fallen.

So, they had a choice to make: either selfishly continue on in their wicked ways or turn and repent for the good of others who would come after them. Clearly, they chose poorly, and Amos could see that choice written on their faces:

Amos 5:16 *Therefore the LORD, the God of hosts, the Lord, saith thus; Wailing shall be in all streets; and they shall say in all the highways, Alas! alas! and they shall call the husbandman to mourning, and such as are skilful of lamentation to wailing.* **17** *And in all vineyards shall be wailing: for I will pass through thee, saith the LORD.*

In nearly countless verses of Scripture, God will refer to Himself or have others refer to Him by a single name. In quite a few verses of Scripture, He will refer to Himself or have His prophets refer to Him by two or more names. But when you see something like you see here, God having Amos refer to Him by three names in a single verse, it should very much catch your attention, as it was designed to catch theirs.

God knew that the people had no intention of following His instruction to *Hate the evil, and love the good, and establish judgment in the gate*. Thus, it is that as He begins verse sixteen, it is with the words *the LORD, the God of hosts, the Lord*. All of that means *Jehovah* [the self-existent God], *Elohim Tsabah* [The Godhead and God of armies], *Adonai* [The lord].

If it seems that He was intent on them fearing, trembling, and being reverent before Him, it is because that is exactly what He intended.

That God said *Therefore* [because you refuse to obey Me in this] *wailing shall be in all streets; and they shall say in all the highways, Alas! alas! and they shall call the husbandman to mourning, and such as are skilful of lamentation to wailing. And in all vineyards shall be wailing: for I will pass through thee, saith the LORD.*

Wailing was about to be heard, and it would be heard throughout the land. The streets, all of them, referring to the broad, open places and ways within a city, would be filled with it. The highways, meaning the areas and roads outside of the cities, would be filled with it as well.

"Alas! Alas!" would be the cry. And as with our anguished "Oh!", it was more of a sound than a word, a mournful cry rather than a meaningful communication.

The husbandmen, meaning those who tended the vine, would be called to mourning. The produce of the land was destroyed or dying, and those who gave their lives and efforts to produce it and harvest its fruit would have nothing to celebrate and no reason for hope to be seen on the withering vines.

At the end of verse sixteen, God told them to call *such as are skilful of lamentation to wailing*. More ominous words could hardly be spoken; those *skilful of lamentation* referred to professional mourners, people who would wail for the dead. These, who were called for funerals, were now, in essence, being called to wail at the funeral of an entire kingdom.

Verse seventeen ends with God saying, *And in all vineyards shall be wailing: for I will pass through thee, saith the LORD.*

If you have read your Bible very much, you may get a bad feeling about God saying that He is going to *pass through*. If you do, it is for good reason. God passing over [Exodus 12:13, 12:23] or passing by [Exodus 34:6; Ezekiel 16:8] tended to be a positive thing. But God passing through was not usually a good thing at all:

Exodus 12:12 *For I will **pass through** the land of Egypt this night, and will **smite** all the firstborn in the land of Egypt,* both man and beast; and against all the gods of Egypt I will **execute judgment**: I am the LORD.

Exodus 12:23 *For the LORD will **pass through** to **smite** the Egyptians; and when he seeth the blood upon the lintel, and on the two side posts, the LORD will pass over the door, and will not suffer the **destroyer** to come in unto your houses to **smite** you.*

When we read in Amos 5:17 that God intended to pass through and that the result would be wailing, it was a very bad consequence brought on by their very bad choices.

A terrifying desire

Amos 5:18 *Woe unto you that desire the day of the LORD! to what end is it for you? the day of the LORD is darkness, and not light.*

When we, in our Christian circles, speak of the day of the LORD, the terminology is old and very familiar to us. But you need to understand that there is a stark dividing line in Scripture before which there are no mentions of it by name. It only appears twenty-five times in Scripture, and it was actually very new to Amos's day; the very first mention of it is from the prophet Isaiah, who was a contemporary of Amos:

Isaiah 2:12 *For the day of the LORD of hosts shall be upon every one that is proud and lofty, and upon every one that is lifted up; and he shall be brought low:*

Amos was listening to people in his day wishing for the day of the LORD. They somehow viewed it as God swooping down and destroying all of their enemies and setting them up high on a pedestal as His fair-haired, favored children.

To put it mildly, they didn't have a clue. The day of the LORD, as it refers to the last days, will indeed see, among other things, God forever deal with all of the enemies of Israel. However, as it applied to their day, it was going to affect them just as much as it would anyone else. Again, Amos put it this way to them: *Woe unto you that desire the day of the LORD! to what end is it for you? the day of the LORD is darkness, and not light.*

They were expecting the day of the LORD to bring them sunshine; it was going to bring bitter darkness. He goes on to describe that in the next two verses:

Amos 5:19 *As if a man did flee from a lion, and a bear met him; or went into the house, and leaned his hand on the wall, and a serpent bit him.* **20** *Shall not the day of the LORD be darkness, and not light? even very dark, and no brightness in it?*

Picture a day like this. You are going about your business, and you happen to run smack-dab into a ravenous lion that is clearly intent on eating you. You, of course, run for your life. And somehow, against the odds, it seems as if you are going to escape! You know if you can just make it around that next corner, you are home free. Giving every bit of effort left in your body, you sprint with all of your might and make it around the corner—and run right into a gigantic, hungry bear, who then rips you apart and eats you.

Or, picture a similar day, but one that goes like this. You are going about your business, and you happen to run smack-dab into a ravenous lion that is clearly intent on eating you. You, of course, run for your life. And somehow, against the odds, it seems as if you are going to escape! You know if you can just make it home, you will be home free. You make one final desperate sprint, burst inside your door, and lock in behind you. Then, trying to catch your breath, you stretch out your hand and lean against the wall—and the deadly snake that was curled up and hiding on the key shelf strikes and kills you.

This is how Amos described the day of the LORD: one divinely appointed disaster after another, with no safe place to run or hide. And this is what it was going to be like for Israel when their near-term day of the LORD hit in the form of the Assyrian army that was going to kill their nation. It would be so bad that Amos described it this way: *Shall not the day of the LORD be darkness, and not light? even very dark, and no brightness in it?*

There would not be a bright spot anywhere in any of it. As it turns out, refusing God's offer of mercy is a terrible idea.

A trashy devotion

Amos 5:21 *I hate, I despise your feast days, and I will not smell in your solemn assemblies.*

This was God speaking to His people. And His words would seem so odd if we had not already seen Him express this exact same sentiment repeatedly in the prophetical writings.

He said that He hated, He despised their feast days and would not smell in their solemn assemblies. And by joining *I hate* and *I despise* together without a conjunction, He was expressing an extra measure of disgust in all of this. What makes this so counterintuitive is that God Himself instituted those feast days for them.

So, what happened? For starters, these feast days held in Bethel were in the wrong place and with the wrong gods. Rather than travel to the Temple in Jerusalem to worship Jehovah, they took the feasts of Jehovah, rebranded them, and mixed them in with their worship of the golden calves and other idols, and they expected God to be happy with all of it since they still gave lip service to Him within all of that abominable mess.

In this, they very much became the forerunners in spirit of much modern worldly evangelicalism of today that embraces every form of wickedness and still expects God to be pleased since they drag the precious name of Jesus into all of their heresy and debauchery.

God went on in verse twenty-one to say: *and I will not smell in your solemn assemblies.*

This presents a sad but somewhat hilarious picture. Early on in Scripture, true followers of God began to incorporate fragrances into worship:

Genesis 8:20 *And Noah builded an altar unto the LORD; and took of every clean beast, and of every clean fowl, and offered burnt offerings on the altar.* **21** *And the LORD* **smelled a sweet savour***; and the LORD said in his heart, I will not again curse the ground any more for man's sake; for the imagination of man's heart is evil from his youth; neither will I again smite any more every thing living, as I have done.*

God went on to heavily incorporate that into the worship of the Tabernacle and Temple:

Exodus 30:34 *And the LORD said unto Moses, Take unto thee sweet spices, stacte, and onycha, and galbanum; these sweet spices with pure frankincense: of each shall there be a like weight:* **35** *And thou shalt make it a perfume, a confection after the art of the apothecary, tempered together, pure and holy:* **36** *And thou shalt beat some of it very small, and put of it before the testimony in the tabernacle of the congregation, where I will meet with thee: it shall be unto you most holy.*

But by Amos's day, God said: *I will not smell in your solemn assemblies.* It means exactly what it sounds like. God held His nose and refused to smell what they were offering. They thought that because they called for a "solemn assembly" and made a pretty-smelling incense to burn, God would take a deep sniff and say, "Wow! I was really angry at all of your sin and wickedness, but that smells so good... let's just forget all about Me being angry. Carry on with what you have been doing."

Instead, God was holding His nose because, as far as He was concerned, they stunk, their incense stunk, and their behavior stunk.

Amos 5:22 *Though ye offer me burnt offerings and your meat offerings, I will not accept them: neither will I regard the peace offerings of your fat beasts.*

As the people viewed the coming calamity and "got a little religion to try and fix things," they brought three types of offerings to the LORD, all of which were mentioned in the law.

Burnt offerings [from the word *olah*, meaning *to go up*] were first. Here is the first place they were mentioned in the law:

Exodus 20:24 *An altar of earth thou shalt make unto me, and shalt sacrifice thereon thy burnt offerings, and thy peace offerings, thy sheep, and thine oxen: in all places where I record my name I will come unto thee, and I will bless thee.*

The first time they were mentioned in singular form tells us what they were:

Exodus 29:18 *And thou shalt burn the whole ram upon the altar: it is a burnt offering unto the LORD: it is a sweet savour, an offering made by fire unto the LORD.*

In a burnt offering, a whole animal would be put upon the altar and burned, sending the smoke upward to the LORD. The International Bible Encyclopedia says that this "was perhaps the most solemn of the sacrifices, and symbolized worship in the full sense, i.e. adoration, devotion, dedication, supplication, and at times expiation [making amends for wrongdoing]." (Orr, 4, 2638)

Meat offerings [from the word *minhah*, indicating a token of friendship] were next. And contrary to the way we view the word meat, when they used it, it normally referred to a grain of some kind. There were a great many of these meat, or meal, offerings in the law and in Israel's history.

Peace offerings of fat beasts were next. This is from the word *shelem* and is related to the word *shalom*. It was a sacrifice that called for peaceable relations between God and man. The fat beasts were prized and valuable creatures that were given up in favor of that hoped-for peaceful relationship.

All of these were straight from the law of Moses, and yet God said that He would not accept or regard any of them. Those two words [from *ratsah* and *nabat*] mean to be pleased with and to look at. God was telling them that no matter how fat and full their offerings were, He despised them and would not even dignify them with a glance in their direction.

Amos 5:23 *Take thou away from me the noise of thy songs; for I will not hear the melody of thy viols.*

God dealt with their fragrances and their sacrifices, and now He takes aim at their music, another vital part of their worship. Like Ezekiel (Ezekiel 26:13), God, through Amos, calls their music *noise.* In neither of those prophetical references is that a complimentary thing. It is not a *ruwah,* a joyful noise as is mentioned seven times in the Old Testament; it is a *hawmoan,* a roar, a tumult, and God said, "Take it away!"

He said, *I will not hear the melody of thy viols.* The instrument called the viol is only spoken of in Isaiah and Amos, and it was something like a harp or a guitar. It made a melody; God was not in the least interested in hearing that melody.

At this point, you can almost hear them in exasperation, saying, "If you don't want sacrifices or fragrances or music, what do you want?"

Here was the answer:

Amos 5:24 *But let judgment run down as waters, and righteousness as a mighty stream.*

I love Adam Clarke's uncharacteristically poetic paraphrase of this verse:

"Let the execution of justice be everywhere like the showers that fall upon the land to render it fertile; and let righteousness in heart and life be like a mighty river, or the Jordan, that shall wind its course through the whole nation, and carry every abomination into the Dead Sea. Let justice and righteousness prevail everywhere, and sweep their contraries out of the land." (Clarke, 4:682)

If I may add my very short and to-the-point paraphrase, it would be "Just do right *before* Me and *to* others."

Jesus would give much the same thought many years later in His ministry:

Matthew 22:37 *Jesus said unto him, Thou shalt love the Lord thy God with all thy heart, and with all thy soul, and with all thy mind.* **38** *This is the first and great commandment.* **39** *And the second is like unto it, Thou shalt love thy neighbour as thyself.* **40** *On these two commandments hang all the law and the prophets.*

What good are sacrifices and sweet smells and singing when we are sinning against God and slighting those around us? I get genuinely weary of people who think that dressing right and putting on a good show in church gives them a pass on living like devils and cutting others to ribbons. That is the very kind of thing God was seeing in Israel in the days of Amos that made Him say, "I hate, I despise your feast days, your fragrances stink to me, I'm not accepting your offerings, and get that 'worship music' out of here."

Amos 5:25 *Have ye offered unto me sacrifices and offerings in the wilderness forty years, O house of Israel?* **26** *But ye have borne the tabernacle of your Moloch and Chiun your images, the star of your god, which ye made to yourselves.* **27** *Therefore will I cause you to go into captivity beyond Damascus, saith the LORD, whose name is The God of hosts.*

The question of verse twenty-five, if put in our vernacular, would have something of a "really" in it. In other words, "Have you *really* offered sacrifices to me, O house of Israel?" We know this because He immediately answers His own question, saying, *But ye have borne the tabernacle of your*

Moloch and Chiun your images, the star of your god, which ye made to yourselves.

Moloch, sometimes referred to as Molech or Milcom, was a god of the Ammonites that required infant sacrifice by fire. Chiun was the Assyrian/Babylonian god, Saturn, and the star was a graven star on the head of any image that would represent Saturn.

This mention of the wilderness and of forty years leads to some interesting questions. I will tell you right up front that almost all commentators believe that this refers to the forty years of wilderness wandering between the time that the children of Israel came out of Egypt until the time that they finally crossed over into the Promised Land.

I do not believe that to be the case at all. To begin with, God in the book of Amos has been ripping Israel to shreds for all of the wickedness they were right then presently engaged in, and there was a ton of it. Why then would He need to suddenly and inexplicably start referring back to something that happened nearly eight hundred years before?

Second, if they had not only been worshipping Moloch and Chiun and the star of their god but even carrying the tabernacle for them, do you think that Moses would have turned a blind eye to it and that God would simply have allowed it, said nothing about it for all forty years nor in any of the years that followed, and then eight hundred years later suddenly said, "Oh, and about that Moloch and Chiun worship eight centuries ago, I am livid about it and I am going to judge you for it!"

Third, these forty years of idol worship were one of the specific reasons He made up His mind to send them into captivity, saying in verse twenty-seven, *Therefore will I cause you to go into captivity beyond Damascus, saith the LORD, whose name is The God of hosts.* If it were Israel's sin in the wilderness this referred to, not only was that generation no longer alive to be punished, but two participating tribes were left out of the judgment, namely Judah and Benjamin, who were now part of the Southern Kingdom.

The more logical supposition is that this was referring to the last forty years of Israel's history as Amos wrote this, especially considering that their king, Jeroboam II, reigned for forty-one years, and Amos seems to have been writing the last few chapters of his book near the end of that time.

Regardless, for their idolatry, among other sins, God determined to send them away into captivity *beyond Damascus*. And the people knew what that meant; if you were going from Israel through Damascus, Syria, you were heading to the last place anyone ever wanted to go:

Assyria.

They asked for the day of the LORD.

They asked and went looking for Assyrian gods, like Chiun.

So the real God was going to send them their near-term day of the LORD; He was going to wreck them and send them to a place where Chiun could easily be found.

Be careful what you ask for; you may just get it.

Chapter Eleven
Don't Rest Easy

Amos 6:1 *Woe to them that are at ease in Zion, and trust in the mountain of Samaria, which are named chief of the nations, to whom the house of Israel came!* **2** *Pass ye unto Calneh, and see; and from thence go ye to Hamath the great: then go down to Gath of the Philistines: be they better than these kingdoms? or their border greater than your border?* **3** *Ye that put far away the evil day, and cause the seat of violence to come near;* **4** *That lie upon beds of ivory, and stretch themselves upon their couches, and eat the lambs out of the flock, and the calves out of the midst of the stall;* **5** *That chant to the sound of the viol, and invent to themselves instruments of musick, like David;* **6** *That drink wine in bowls, and anoint themselves with the chief ointments: but they are not grieved for the affliction of Joseph.* **7** *Therefore now shall they go captive with the first that go captive, and the banquet of them that stretched themselves shall be removed.* **8** *The Lord GOD hath sworn by himself, saith the LORD the God of hosts, I abhor the excellency of Jacob, and hate his palaces: therefore will I deliver up the city with all that is therein.* **9** *And it shall come to pass, if there remain ten men in one house, that they shall die.* **10** *And a man's uncle shall take him up, and he that burneth him, to bring out the bones out of the house, and shall say unto him that is by the sides of the house, Is there yet any with thee? and he shall say, No. Then shall he* *say, Hold thy tongue: for we may not make mention of the name of the LORD.* **11** *For, behold, the LORD commandeth, and he will smite the great house with breaches, and the little house with clefts.* **12** *Shall horses run upon the rock? will one plow there with oxen? for ye have turned judgment into gall, and the fruit of righteousness into hemlock:* **13** *Ye which rejoice in a thing of nought, which say, Have we not taken to us horns by our own strength?* **14** *But, behold, I will raise up against you a nation, O house of Israel, saith the LORD the God of hosts; and they shall afflict you from the entering in of Hemath unto the river of the wilderness.*

Amazingly, the children of Israel had been asking for and longing for the day of the LORD, heedless of the fact that when it came, it was going to be a disaster for them. Seeing this, Amos pointed out the flaws in their thinking and showed them how foolish they were for assuming that they were God's fair-haired children and that He would never judge them in spite of their wickedness and rampant idolatry.

He is continuing along that same line of thinking here in Amos 6.

A silly comfort

Amos 6:1 *Woe to them that are at ease in Zion, and trust in the mountain of Samaria, which are named chief of the nations, to whom the house of Israel came!*

We need to begin by identifying the recipients of this portion of Amos's prophecy. Those recipients were both the Northern and the Southern Kingdoms, both Israel and Judah. We see this in references to both Zion and the mountains of Samaria. Zion was a name for Jerusalem, the capital of the Southern Kingdom, a city on a mountain. Samaria was the capital of the Northern Kingdom of Israel and was also on a mountain. In fact, its name means "Watch Mountain." So, while Amos was sent mostly to Israel, he, like many of the other prophets, also very often took time to deal with Judah as well.

As to the message itself, with just a small number of exceptions, when the prophets spoke of those who were at ease, it was a very negative thing. And in this case, especially since the verse begins with the word *woe*, the second time in ten verses (Amos 5:18) that he has used it, it was clearly a negative thing.

God said *Woe to them that are at ease in Zion*. The phrase *at ease* means "secure, careless, arrogant." In our terms, they were quite certain that they could not be taken. Like King Belshazzar of the Babylonians in Daniel 5, they believed that their position was unassailable and would not hesitate to insult God Himself, confident that even He could not cause them to be brought low.

And why were they so confident? We find that answer in the words *and trust in the mountain of Samaria, which are named chief of the nations, *to whom the house of Israel came!* [*when they entered into Canaan as their Promised Land]

Both the mountains of the North and the mountains of the South, both of the capital cities, were famous. Reflecting on Amos's description of them as being *named chief of the nations*, Clarke said, "The mountain of Zion, and the mountain of Samaria, were considered the chief or most celebrated among the nations, as the two kingdoms to which they belonged were the most distinguished on the earth." (Clarke, 4:683)

Especially when we consider the Temple that was still standing on the mountain there in Jerusalem, it is easy to see why the people would look to their respective mountains, their respective glory, their respective success, breathe an easy sigh of relief, and say in so many words, "We are far too pretty for God to ever judge."

They were about to learn differently:

Amos 6:2 *Pass ye unto Calneh, and see; and from thence go ye to Hamath the great: then go down to Gath of the Philistines: be they better than these kingdoms? or their border greater than your border?*

Calneh was once a very powerful city located on the east bank of the Tigris River. But very recently to Amos's day, it had been conquered and subjugated by Syria. (Jamieson, 2:549) God told them to take a trip down there to see it.

From there, they were to move the field trip to Hamath the Great. Hamath was a very prominent and powerful city on the Orontes River in Syria. And yet, Israel's own king currently on the throne, Jeroboam II, had just recently wrecked and subjugated it (1 Kings 14:25). But shortly after that, it was wrecked yet again by Assyria (2 Kings 18:34).

The field trip had one more stop. God told them they next needed to *go down to Gath of the Philistines.* And the reason He told them to do that was because Gath, one of the five most prominent and powerful cities of the Philistines, had also been wrecked, this time by King Uzziah of Judah (2 Chronicles 26:6).

Here was God's point: *be they* [Calneh, Hamath, Gath] *better than these kingdoms* [Israel and Judah]*? or their* [Calneh, Hamath, Gath's] *border greater than your border?*

These words bear a bit of an explanation, lest we inadvertently take them backward in their meaning. We would expect God to say, "Are you better than those kingdoms? Is your border greater than their border? No, and yet they fell, so you will, too." Instead, we find the opposite question, "Are they, Calneh and Hamath and Gath, better than these kingdoms, the kingdoms of Israel and Judah? Is their border greater than your border?" That sounds a bit like God was saying, "They were weaker than you, so they fell." But that is the exact opposite of the message He was sending.

The mistake we are at risk of making is missing the little words *be they,* or in our vernacular, "are they?" In other words, are those three kingdoms presently stronger and greater than you? And the expected answer is, "No, they currently are not." But here is what everyone understood: they used to be. They once had far stronger borders, fortresses, and military might than both Israel and Judah. And yet, all of them had fallen. The mental field trip God was asking them to make, then, was to demonstrate that if far stronger nations had fallen to the Assyrian scourge, Israel and Judah were at risk of the exact same thing since they had forsaken the one true God in favor of the gods of all of those nations who had already fallen.

Amos 6:3 *Ye that put far away the evil day, and cause the seat of violence to come near;* **4** *That lie upon beds of ivory, and stretch themselves upon their couches, and eat the lambs out of the flock, and the calves out of the midst of the stall;* **5** *That chant to the sound of the viol, and invent to themselves instruments of musick, like David;* **6** *That drink wine in bowls, and anoint themselves with the chief ointments: but they are not grieved for the affliction of Joseph.*

These four verses form one long sentence, a sentence in which God describes the soft luxury people were living in, all while the prophesied destruction was heading their direction.

The first description He gave of them was: *Ye that put far away the evil day, and cause the seat of violence to come near.* What He means by this is that the very day of judgment, which was near and beating down on them, they put far away, meaning they postdated it by years or decades or centuries and said that it would not happen anytime soon. They were like criminals on death row who believe they will be able to appeal themselves into a ripe old age, heedless of the fact that their execution is firmly scheduled for the end of the week.

Israel vainly believing this, motivated them to *cause the seat of violence to come near*. In other words, as He has been castigating them for throughout the book, they were turning the court system into a pay-for-play system that ran roughshod over the weak and poor. Their belief that judgment would never come was making them embrace that *seat of violence* system.

His second description of them was: *That lie upon beds of ivory, and stretch themselves upon their couches*. The beds of ivory were elaborate, ornamental beds inlaid with ivory and other materials, such as mother-of-pearl. The couches were also items of luxury. His description is of people who were literally lying in the lap of luxury while judgment was bearing down on them.

His third description of them was: *and eat the lambs out of the flock, and the calves out of the midst of the stall*. This was a way of describing the very best of the herds and the tenderest of the meat. They were eating very, very well, saving nothing, heedless of the siege and starvation they were facing.

His fourth description of them was: *That chant to the sound of the viol, and invent to themselves instruments of musick, like David*. In his lifetime, David had not just been a singer and musician; he was also the creator and fabricator of musical instruments. He invented new instruments to use in the worship of God:

1 Chronicles 23:5 *Moreover four thousand were porters; and four thousand praised the LORD with the instruments which I made, said David, to praise therewith.*

So, was there anything wrong with inventing musical instruments, using them in worship, and chanting along with the viol, which David himself doubtless did as well? Certainly not. But David did all of this while actually worshipping the LORD and therefore helping to bring God's blessings on the nation, not while in active disobedience to the LORD with the LORD about to destroy the entire nation because of that disobedience. What Amos's people were doing was worshipping worship, not worshipping the God that worship is supposed to be given to.

The fifth description He used of them was: *That drink wine in bowls, and anoint themselves with the chief ointments.* This was a further description of their soft, luxurious lifestyle in the face of impending disaster. The bowls they were drinking out of were the large bowls in which the wine was mixed and diluted. The normal practice was to finish mixing that wine, pour it into smaller cups, and then drink from the cups. But they simply slurped it from the bowl to show that they feared no lack and needed to show no restraint.

The chief ointments they were anointing themselves with were precious oils and perfumes, extremely costly substances. This was yet another instance in which they were using their resources for lavish luxury, truly believing that no harm could or would befall them.

The final description He gives of them is designed to be much like a gut punch, knocking the pompous air out of them:

...but they are not grieved for the affliction of Joseph.

God had already very plainly told them that disaster was coming and that they (Joseph, put here for Israel) were going to fall. He had told them that the nation was going to die. But rather than show the proper response—grief, sorrow, and repentance—they chose to soak themselves in sensuality and to assuage all their fears with amusement.

They were very much at ease—and that was not going to end well for them.

A silent choice

Amos 6:7 *Therefore* [because they are at ease while disaster approaches] *now shall they go captive with the first that* *go captive, and the banquet of them that stretched themselves shall be removed.*

The people that were being described in the first six verses, as with so much that we see in Amos's prophecy, were the leaders of the people. They were the ones in charge, the ones who were supposed to be taking care of everyone and leading them right. But instead, in spite of the warnings, they were living luxuriously. So God said *therefore*, because of this, they would go into captivity with the very first group of people to go into captivity. In fact, their captivity would come in the midst of their banqueting; they would be taken straight from their revelry to their ruin.

Amos 6:8 *The Lord GOD hath sworn by himself, saith the LORD the God of hosts, I abhor the excellency of Jacob, and hate his palaces: therefore will I deliver up the city with all that is therein.*

When human beings want to swear an oath, they do it on something viewed as greater than themselves: the Bible, Mama's grave, or some other significant thing. But when God swears an oath, He doesn't have that luxury. That being the case, the most significant oath He can swear is *The Lord GOD hath sworn by himself*. "By Himself" is from the word *benaphsho*, from the root word *nephesh*. It means by His very existence. This, therefore, is the most serious of matters.

In this instance, what God was swearing was, *I abhor the excellency of Jacob, and hate his palaces: therefore will I deliver up the city with all that is therein.* To put it mildly, that is a radically different sentiment than was expressed elsewhere:

Psalm 47:4 *He shall choose our inheritance for us, the excellency of Jacob whom he loved. Selah.*

The sin of the people made God despise what He was in the habit of loving and determined to give it and them to their enemies.

Amos 6:9 *And it shall come to pass, if there remain ten men in one house, that they shall die.*

The picture that God begins to paint in this verse, which is completed in the next verse, is stark and sad. The people were going to be besieged; a huge percentage of them would die by the sword. But if by chance ten men somehow managed to escape from the enemy and hide in a house, a house already battered by the enemy, God would make sure that all ten of those men, one hundred percent, would die.

The next verse will infer the how:

Amos 6:10 *And a man's uncle shall take him up, and he that burneth him, to bring out the bones out of the house...*

The fact that the bodies were being burned rather than prepared and buried lets us know that it was a plague that God was promising, a highly communicable, deadly disease to go along with the ravages of the enemy they had already suffered. Further, this plague would take the youngest and strongest; it would be the uncles carrying their nephews away to be burned.

The sad picture continues with the words, *and shall say unto him that is by the sides of the house, Is there yet any with thee? and he shall say, No. Then shall he say, Hold thy tongue: for we may not make mention of the name of the LORD.*

The sides of the house mean the farthest corners; it pictures someone huddling in the very back, trying to hide. The uncle, the older relative who has come to carry out the bodies for burning, sees someone who has come into the house to check on his family and realizes that they are all dead; that someone is huddling in the very back, clearly in shock and terror. The uncle says, "Is there anyone else? Is absolutely anyone left alive?"

The one hiding in the shadows simply says, "No." But then, as he opens his mouth to say something else, the uncle, knowing full well he is about to hear something like "May God have mercy on us!" interrupts him and says, *Hold thy tongue:*

for we may not make mention of the name of the LORD. He then closes with this hopeless addendum:

Amos 6:11 *For, behold, the LORD commandeth, and he will smite the great house with breaches, and the little house with clefts.*

In full, his speech now runs something like this: "Do not mention the name of the LORD, because He is the one who has commanded all of this destruction; all of the great houses are going to end up ripped wide open, and even the little houses will be torn and gashed."

It did not have to be this way, this silence in regard to the name of the LORD. They could have both spoken *of Him* and *to Him*; all they needed to do was repent.

Instead, when it all finally came to pass, they chose the silent treatment.

A senseless complication

Amos 6:12 *Shall horses run upon the rock? will one plow there with oxen? for ye have turned judgment into gall, and the fruit of righteousness into hemlock:* **13** *Ye which rejoice in a thing of nought, which say, Have we not taken to us horns by our own strength?*

These two verses make one sentence, a sentence in which God paints an intentionally ridiculous picture to demonstrate what the people were doing to themselves and the theological thought process behind it all.

He begins by asking, *Shall horses run upon the rock?* The answer was no. This was thousands of years before the iron shoeing of horses; trying to run a horse across rocks would cripple it.

The next question was, *will one plow there* [on the rock] *with oxen?* Once again, the answer is no. The implements would not break the rock; the rock would break the implements. And as with the horses, the oxen would be injured in the attempt.

God quickly explains the intentionally ridiculous word picture, saying: *for ye have turned judgment into gall, and the fruit of righteousness into hemlock.*

This is the same accusation He made against them in Amos 5:7. Like a horse running on rock or oxen plowing on rock, they were putting things together that did not rightly or sensibly go together. They were turning judgment into gall, meaning something bitter and at times even poisonous. They were turning the fruit of righteousness into hemlock, a bitter and poisonous plant. Both judgment and fruit (the fruit of righteousness) were supposed to be sweet to people; they were supposed to look forward to it, knowing it was just. Instead, all of it had been made bitter. And why were they so brazen? Here is why:

Amos 6:13 *Ye which rejoice in a thing of nought, which say, Have we not taken to us horns by our own strength?*

You will find a debate as to whether this referred to their idols or their riches. They had both and trusted both, but in the context of this passage, it is their riches that are being referred to. They thought their prosperity gave them the power (horns and strength) to run over people—and the power for God not to be able to do anything about it.

They really thought they would get by with it; purveyors of injustice anywhere always do. But that was not the way it was going to go:

Amos 6:14 *But, behold, I will raise up against you a nation, O house of Israel, saith the LORD the God of hosts; and they shall afflict you from the entering in of Hemath unto the river of the wilderness.*

By now, the identity of this nation will not come as a surprise to you; God was going to raise Assyria up against His people, Israel. They would afflict Israel from the entering of Hamath, which was their far northern border, all the way to the river of the wilderness, Kedron, which empties into the Dead Sea and at that point marks their far southern border.

They were doomed while they danced and did not even have the sense to realize it.

They were resting easy—without any good reason to do so. No matter how well-off you are, no matter how fat your bank account, no matter how luxurious your life, if you are living a life that makes God say, "I am going to wreck you," you have absolutely no reason to rest easy.

Chapter Twelve
When the Preaching Gets Personal

Amos 7:1 *Thus hath the Lord GOD shewed unto me; and, behold, he formed grasshoppers in the beginning of the shooting up of the latter growth; and, lo, it was the latter growth after the king's mowings.* **2** *And it came to pass, that when they had made an end of eating the grass of the land, then I said, O Lord GOD, forgive, I beseech thee: by whom shall Jacob arise? for he is small.* **3** *The LORD repented for this: It shall not be, saith the LORD.* **4** *Thus hath the Lord GOD shewed unto me: and, behold, the Lord GOD called to contend by fire, and it devoured the great deep, and did eat up a part.* **5** *Then said I, O Lord GOD, cease, I beseech thee: by whom shall Jacob arise? for he is small.* **6** *The LORD repented for this: This also shall not be, saith the Lord GOD.* **7** *Thus he shewed me: and, behold, the Lord stood upon a wall made by a plumbline, with a plumbline in his hand.* **8** *And the LORD said unto me, Amos, what seest thou? And I said, A plumbline. Then said the Lord, Behold, I will set a plumbline in the midst of my people Israel: I will not again pass by them any more:* **9** *And the high places of Isaac shall be desolate, and the sanctuaries of Israel shall be laid waste; and I will rise against the house of Jeroboam with the sword.* **10** *Then Amaziah the priest of Bethel sent to Jeroboam king of Israel, saying, Amos hath conspired against thee in the midst of the house of Israel: the land is not able to* *bear all his words.* **11** *For thus Amos saith, Jeroboam shall die by the sword, and Israel shall surely be led away captive out of their own land.* **12** *Also Amaziah said unto Amos, O thou seer, go, flee thee away into the land of Judah, and there eat bread, and prophesy there:* **13** *But prophesy not again any more at Bethel: for it is the king's chapel, and it is the king's court.* **14** *Then answered Amos, and said to Amaziah, I was no prophet, neither was I a prophet's son; but I was an herdman, and a gatherer of sycomore fruit:* **15** *And the LORD took me as I followed the flock, and the LORD said unto me, Go, prophesy unto my people Israel.* **16** *Now therefore hear thou the word of the LORD: Thou sayest, Prophesy not against Israel, and drop not thy word against the house of Isaac.* **17** *Therefore thus saith the LORD; Thy wife shall be an harlot in the city, and thy sons and thy daughters shall fall by the sword, and thy land shall be divided by line; and thou shalt die in a polluted land: and Israel shall surely go into captivity forth of his land.*

Since the middle of Amos 2, Amos has been ripping into the nation of Israel. The *nation* of Israel. What he has not done, up until this point in his prophecy, is call individual names of people in high places.

That is now going to change in dramatic fashion.

A vanishing patience

Amos 7:1 *Thus hath the Lord GOD shewed unto me; and, behold, he formed grasshoppers in the beginning of the shooting up of the latter growth; and, lo, it was the latter growth after the king's mowings.*

From the first verse in chapter seven through the first verse in chapter eight, Amos is going to use the phrase *thus hath the Lord God shewed* me or a similar phrase four times. God was indeed showing Amos some things, and Israel did not want to see or hear about any of them.

As Amos begins recounting this information, he is telling the people what God has already shown him. He will go on from there in each case to inform the people about the conversation between himself and God that followed each of those revelations.

The first thing God showed him was that He, God, *formed grasshoppers in the beginning of the shooting up of the latter growth; and, lo, it was the latter growth after the king's mowings.*

As is always the case when you see a reference like this, this was a judgment that dealt with the food supply. God was going to make sure that His grasshoppers showed up at the worst possible time to devastate the crops growing in the field.

The king's mowings refer to the very first harvest of the crops; it was a tax that he exacted from the people for his own use, mostly for his livestock. Everyone knew they were going to lose that each year. But by this horde of grasshoppers coming up on the land during the latter growth, the attack was on the food supply of the people themselves, including the king. When Amos saw those grasshoppers at that exact time, he knew how bad it would be. As the vision progressed, his fears proved correct:

Amos 7:2 *And it came to pass, that when they had made an end of eating the grass of the land, then I said, O Lord GOD, forgive, I beseech thee: by whom shall Jacob arise? for he is small.*

In the vision, Amos saw those grasshoppers eat the grass of the land until there was nothing left. This would be an utterly devastating judgment on the land, one that it would not likely recover from. So, Amos interceded on behalf of his people. He begged God to forgive His people. And the basis on which he did so was the mercy of God; He pointed out that Jacob (the nation of Israel) would not be able to rise again from such a calamity.

It is interesting that he closed verse two with the words, *for he is small*. They were actually in one of their more prosperous time periods under the reign of Jeroboam II and had recovered much territory lost under previous kings. But compared to the Assyrian scourge bearing down upon them, and further, compared to the judgment of God that was bearing down upon them for their sin, they were indeed small; any nation is. Amos understood that and thus prayed for his people. And God responded:

Amos 7:3 *The LORD repented for this: It shall not be, saith the LORD.*

As we observe each time we find some form of the word *repent* applied to God in Scripture, it never means of Him that He is acknowledging some sin or sinfulness, for He has none of that in Him. To repent means to turn; when applied to God, it thus means that God has changed His proposed course of action. And as is so often the case with that, this change in God's plans was brought about by the prayers of one of His own, namely Amos.

This obviously makes the notion that God predetermines everything in the universe from before the beginning of time and that our prayers never move Him to change things appear every bit as silly as it actually is. Let the Scripture stand as God has written it: God was going to judge Israel by the grasshoppers, Amos prayed, and God chose to rescind that judgment based on those prayers.

Amos 7:4 *Thus hath the Lord GOD shewed unto me: and, behold, the Lord GOD called to contend by fire, and it devoured the great deep, and did eat up a part.*

The second looming judgment that God showed Amos in a vision was a raging inferno that would wreck the land, going so far as to affect the deepest of their water supply. This, like Elijah's called-for fire on Mount Carmel that licked up the water out of the trench, would be utterly supernatural.

Once again, Amos realized the magnitude of the destruction his people were facing. And once again, he interceded on their behalf:

Amos 7:5 *Then said I, O Lord GOD, cease, I beseech thee: by whom shall Jacob arise? for he is small.*

Amos used the exact same words in the last half of each of his pleas. He wanted God to grant mercy based on the fact that Jacob was small and would never arise from such judgment. The only difference between what we see in verse five and what we see in verse two is that in verse two, Amos asked God to forgive, and in verse five, he asks God to cease.

He meant much the same thing in both of those; he was asking God not to do what God said that He intended to do, which was to destroy Israel. And once again, his prayer made a difference:

Amos 7:6 *The LORD repented for this: This also shall not be, saith the Lord GOD.*

For the second time, God laid out exactly what he intended to do. For the second time, Amos, a human being, prayed and asked Him not to do it. And for the second time, the sovereign God repented, changed His mind on His intended course of action, and chose not to do it.

All of this makes the argument that the sovereignty of God micromanages and predetermines every detail of every activity of everything and everyone in the entire universe bewilderingly unbiblical and illogical. Life is not a marionette show; God designed it in such a way that we have the free will to make choices and that He, who knew it all in advance, is nonetheless moved one way or the other by our choices and by our prayers.

Amos 7:7 *Thus he shewed me: and, behold, the Lord stood upon a wall made by a plumbline, with a plumbline in his hand.*

In the first vision of proposed judgment, God showed Amos grasshoppers. In the second vision of proposed judgment, God showed Amos a raging fire. But neither of those two things could compare with the ominous nature of the third vision in which God showed Amos Himself, standing on a wall that had been made by use of a plumbline ensuring its perfection, with a plumbline in His hand.

At first blush, you may think that I have gotten that backward; how bad could it be when there are no grasshoppers eating all of the food and no fire devouring the land? How bad could it be when it is just God standing on a wall with the simplest of things in His hand?

The answer is very, very bad:

Amos 7:8 *And the LORD said unto me, Amos, what seest thou? And I said, A plumbline. Then said the Lord, Behold, I will set a plumbline in the midst of my people Israel: I will not again pass by them any more:* **9** *And the high places of Isaac shall be desolate, and the sanctuaries of Israel shall be laid waste; and I will rise against the house of Jeroboam with the sword.*

God asked Amos what he saw. Amos answered accurately, replying that he saw the plumbline that was in God's hand. A plumbline is a string with a metal weight attached to the end of it. It is used to mark perfectly straight lines, either for building something or for destroying something.

God then returned this reply: *Behold, I will set a plumbline in the midst of my people Israel: I will not again pass by them any more:*

Two chapters ago, when we were covering the end of Amos 5, I made this observation:

"If you have read your Bible very much, you may get a bad feeling about God saying that He is going to *pass through*. If you do, it is for good reason. God passing over [Exodus 12:13, 12:23] or passing by [Exodus 34:6; Ezekiel 16:8] tended to be a positive thing. But God passing through was not usually a good thing at all." (p 140)

That truth comes into play in this verse, for God has here promised not to pass by His people anymore. He is high and lifted up and determined to set a plumbline in the very midst of them. This marked everyone on every side of the line as fit for and marked for destruction.

Please remember, at this point, that Amos was uttering all of this prophecy publicly. That is very important for you to understand as you see the ending of the sentence in verse nine:

Amos 7:9 *And the high places of Isaac shall be desolate, and the sanctuaries of Israel shall be laid waste; and I will rise against the house of Jeroboam with the sword.*

Amos gave God's words to the people, and in this verse, those words were that the high places of Isaac would be destroyed. That referred to Beersheba, where Isaac in Genesis 26 had built an altar to the Lord. By the days of Jeroboam II, that once-holy place had become a defiled and dirty place, a center of idolatry, a place that God determined to wreck into desolation.

The second part was that the sanctuaries of Israel would be laid waste. Sanctuaries in this place referred both to their idolatrous houses of worship and to their lofty homes, both of which they vainly imagined were safe from God or man. They were wrong, and those sanctuaries would end up desolate, with naught but bugs and beasts to inhabit the rubble.

It was the third part of Amos's words in verse nine, though, that was going to cause the explosion:

...and I will rise against the house of Jeroboam with the sword.

Jeroboam was the king. He was very much alive, very much on the throne, and, like most kings, not planning on going anywhere. God, though, had very different plans. He had withdrawn the judgment of the grasshoppers, He had withdrawn the judgment of the fire, but His patience was now gone, and the judgment of the plumb line would stand and would specifically affect the king on the throne and all of his household.

As I noted, though, please remember that Amos spoke these words publicly. That is about to become very important.

A vitriolic protest

Amos 7:10 *Then Amaziah the priest of Bethel sent to Jeroboam king of Israel, saying, Amos hath conspired against thee in the midst of the house of Israel: the land is not able to bear all his words.* **11** *For thus Amos saith, Jeroboam shall die by the sword, and Israel shall surely be led away captive out of their own land.*

We are introduced here to the antagonist of the book, Amaziah, the priest of Bethel. He has the most ironic of names; Amaziah means "Jehovah is mighty." Apparently, not mighty enough for Amaziah, though; we find here that he was the priest of Bethel, where the golden calf was housed. Amaziah was a priest to a false god, an idol made by human hands. He was the religious puppet of the king on the throne and entirely beholden to the financial support of Jeroboam's idolatrous system.

Little wonder, then, that when he heard Amos's prophecy, he immediately sent word to the king, saying, *Amos hath conspired against thee in the midst of the house of Israel: the land is not able to bear all his words.*

Amaziah's accusation was completely untrue, as will be the case with most of the rest of his words against Amos. Amos had not conspired against the king or anyone else; Amos simply delivered the word of God as God gave it to him to deliver. Amaziah may not have liked the mail, but Amos was merely the deliveryman, not the author.

Amaziah told the king, *the land is not able to bear all his words*. That was also entirely untrue. The land not only could have borne his words, it should have borne his words; no good is ever done by listening to soothing lies rather than painful truths.

Amaziah then leveled this accusation against Amos:

Amos 7:11 *For thus Amos saith, Jeroboam shall die by the sword, and Israel shall surely be led away captive out of their own land.*

This accusation was a subtle mixture of truth and lies. Amos never said that Jeroboam would be killed with the sword; he said that God would rise against *the house* of Jeroboam with a sword. That may or may not have included Jeroboam himself, and it may or may not have even been in Jeroboam's day. The last part of the accusation, though, the claim that Amos had prophesied that Israel would be carried captive in a foreign land, certainly was true, as we saw in Amos 6:7.

Regardless, Amaziah tattled his muddled mixture of truth and lies and then turned to deliver his own word to Amos:

Amos 7:12 *Also Amaziah said unto Amos, O thou seer, go, flee thee away into the land of Judah, and there eat bread, and prophesy there:* **13** *But prophesy not again any more at Bethel: for it is the king's chapel, and it is the king's court.*

When Amaziah referred to Amos as a *seer*, meaning a prophet, please hear and read the sarcasm in that title. This was not a term of respect coming off his lips; it was dripping and seething with disdain.

Amaziah told Amos, who was a resident of the Southern Kingdom of Judah, to run like a scared little child back to the land of Judah and eat his bread and do his prophesying there. That was his way of saying, "Go earn your living and do your preaching back home; you aren't wanted here." And he backed up that meaning by then saying, *But prophesy not again any more at Bethel: for it is the king's chapel, and it is the king's court.*

The word chapel is a fairly common word in our day, especially in Christian circles. All Christian schools have chapel services, Bible colleges have chapel services, churches have prayer chapels, and so on. But this marks the only usage of the English word chapel in the entire Bible. It comes from the word *miqdash,* which is the same word that in verse nine is rendered *sanctuaries.*

Bethel was indeed the king's chapel, his sanctuary for worship. And Amaziah did not want Amos causing any trouble there with pesky things like the truth and the Word of God.

Bethel was also, at the same time it was the king's sanctuary, *the king's court.* Jamieson, Fausset and Brown observed that this meant it was the "residence: the seat of empire, where the king holds his court, and which thou oughtest to have reverenced. Samaria was the usual king's residence: but for the convenience of attending the calf-worship, a royal palace was at Beth-el also." (Jamieson, 2:555)

This lets us know that all the while Amos was prophesying against the king and the kingdom there in Bethel, he was doing so in the king's front yard. And the king was very clearly home since Amaziah had no trouble running back and forth between Amos and the king with his tattling and with his threats. Talk about godly guts on the part of Amos!

A vicious pushback

Amaziah's words to Amos were a not-at-all thinly veiled threat. And Amos, a true man of God if there ever was one, was not going to shrink back from it

Amos 7:14 *Then answered Amos, and said to Amaziah, I was no prophet, neither was I a prophet's son; but I was an herdman, and a gatherer of sycomore fruit:* **15** *And the LORD took me as I followed the flock, and the LORD said unto me, Go, prophesy unto my people Israel.*

Here is what I showed you about Amos when we first began to study this minor prophet:

> "As to occupation, we find here that Amos was of the herdsmen of Tekoa. Amos was from Judah, the Southern Kingdom. Tekoa was 6 miles south of Bethlehem in a rugged yet beautiful region of the land. Amos really was 'from the sticks,' in our vernacular. He tended sheep out there in Tekoa. And as we will find in chapter seven of the book, he was also employed in gathering sycamore fruit." (p 72)

We have now come to that point. Amaziah has disdainfully called Amos a seer and told him to run back home to Judah like a scared little child. In response, Amos said, *I was no prophet, neither was I a prophet's son; but I was an herdman, and a gatherer of sycomore fruit: And the LORD took me as I followed the flock, and the LORD said unto me, Go, prophesy unto my people Israel.*

In our terms, Amos just told Amaziah something like this: "Prophet? Is that what you think I am? You really don't have a clue, Sparky. I have never been a clergy kind of guy; I have spent my life outdoors, working my fingers to the bone. The only reason I am prophesying here now is because God came and told me to do so. So, if you plan on scaring me, you better be bigger and badder than the wolves and lions and bears and robbers I have spent my life dealing with, because this hillbilly preacher is going to keep right on obeying God whether you like it or not."

But Amos was not done yet, not by a long shot. And Amaziah was about to rue the day he ever threatened Amos:

Amos 7:16 *Now therefore hear thou the word of the LORD: Thou sayest, Prophesy not against Israel, and drop not thy word against the house of Isaac.* **17** *Therefore thus saith the LORD; Thy wife shall be an harlot in the city, and thy sons and thy daughters shall fall by the sword, and thy land shall be divided by line; and thou shalt die in a polluted land: and Israel shall surely go into captivity forth of his land.*

Amaziah had told Amos in no uncertain terms not to prophesy against Israel and not to drop his word of judgment against the house of Isaac, meaning the Northern Kingdom. In so doing, he was standing against God Himself, who commanded Amos to do what he was doing. Because of that, Amos's next words, at God's command, were: *Therefore thus saith the LORD; Thy wife shall be an harlot in the city, and thy sons and thy daughters shall fall by the sword, and thy land shall be divided by line; and thou shalt die in a polluted land: and Israel shall surely go into captivity forth of his land.*

Five gut-punches, back-to-back-to-back-to-back-to-back.

When Assyria finally stormed into the kingdom, Amaziah's own wife would be turned into a prostitute. The sensual worship of the idols that they voluntarily and enthusiastically participated in would now become compulsory at the hands of that enemy.

Amaziah's own children would die by the sword.

Israel would be divided by line, divvied up and given away as trinkets to those loyal to Assyria.

Amaziah himself would be carried away captive into a dirty, polluted land never to return.

Israel would be carried away into captivity.

And in this instance, it was *therefore;* it was because Amaziah stood against him. When ordinary people stand against God and righteousness, the backlash will likely not be this severe. But when the clergy, those charged with watching for the souls of the people, are instead those who try to keep the truth from the people, the judgment will be swift and severe.

You may not particularly like it, but it is wise not to get upset when the message of God through His man gets very personal.

Chapter Thirteen
From The Fruit To The Famine

Amos 8:1 *Thus hath the Lord GOD shewed unto me: and behold a basket of summer fruit.* **2** *And he said, Amos, what seest thou? And I said, A basket of summer fruit. Then said the LORD unto me, The end is come upon my people of Israel; I will not again pass by them any more.* **3** *And the songs of the temple shall be howlings in that day, saith the Lord GOD: there shall be many dead bodies in every place; they shall cast them forth with silence.* **4** *Hear this, O ye that swallow up the needy, even to make the poor of the land to fail,* **5** *Saying, When will the new moon be gone, that we may sell corn? and the sabbath, that we may set forth wheat, making the ephah small, and the shekel great, and falsifying the balances by deceit?* **6** *That we may buy the poor for silver, and the needy for a pair of shoes; yea, and sell the refuse of the wheat?* **7** *The LORD hath sworn by the excellency of Jacob, Surely I will never forget any of their works.* **8** *Shall not the land tremble for this, and every one mourn that dwelleth therein? and it shall rise up wholly as a flood; and it shall be cast out and drowned, as by the flood of Egypt.* **9** *And it shall come to pass in that day, saith the Lord GOD, that I will cause the sun to go down at noon, and I will darken the earth in the clear day:* **10** *And I will turn your feasts into mourning, and all your songs into lamentation; and I will bring up sackcloth upon all loins, and baldness upon every head; and I will make it* *as the mourning of an only son, and the end thereof as a bitter day.* **11** *Behold, the days come, saith the Lord GOD, that I will send a famine in the land, not a famine of bread, nor a thirst for water, but of hearing the words of the LORD:* **12** *And they shall wander from sea to sea, and from the north even to the east, they shall run to and fro to seek the word of the LORD, and shall not find it.* **13** *In that day shall the fair virgins and young men faint for thirst.* **14** *They that swear by the sin of Samaria, and say, Thy god, O Dan, liveth; and, The manner of Beersheba liveth; even they shall fall, and never rise up again.*

At the end of chapter seven, Amos had his confrontation with Amaziah. Interestingly, after Amos told him what was going to happen to him and his wife and his children and his king and his kingdom, Amaziah is not heard from again for the entire rest of the book. It seems very much like Amaziah was not used to dealing with people who were not scared and would not back down.

But Amos was still not done; he picked right back up where he left off, prophesying against Israel. And in chapter eight, he will begin that prophecy with fruit and end it with a famine.

A basket of fruit

Amos 8:1 *Thus hath the Lord GOD shewed unto me: and behold a basket of summer fruit.*

Several different times in chapter seven, Amos uttered some form of the words, *thus hath God shewed me.* He does so once again to start the prophecy of chapter eight. What he saw in this particular vision was a basket of summer fruit; the summer fruit was that which was harvested at the very end of summer, right before fall, and signified the coming deadness of winter.

God begins a play on words in this verse that He will culminate in the next verse. The word for summer fruit is *qayitz*; keep that in mind for a moment as we begin to look at the next verse.

Amos 8:2 *And he said, Amos, what seest thou? And I said, A basket of summer fruit. Then said the LORD unto me, The end is come upon my people of Israel; I will not again pass by them any more.*

God showed Amos the vision and then asked Amos what he saw. Amos answered correctly: *A basket of summer fruit.* A basket of *qayitz*. God then responded: *The end is come upon my people of Israel; I will not again pass by them any more.*

The word *end* is from *qets*. It is a closely related and intentionally similar-sounding word to *qayitz*. God showed Amos the basket of summer fruit, which marked the end of summer and the beginning of the deadness of winter, and in so many words, said, "Just like that, I am also going to end Israel. You see *qayitz*, and I am bringing a *qetz*."

God would no longer pass by His people. As we have been observing in this study, God passing by in Scripture was generally a sign of blessings from His hand and very good things from His heart. But because Israel pushed Him away with their repeated idolatry, God determined not to come their way with His blessings anymore.

The result of that absence and end would not be good:

Amos 8:3 *And the songs of the temple shall be howlings in that day, saith the Lord GOD: there shall be many dead bodies in every place; they shall cast them forth with silence.*

The progression of this verse is absolutely devastating. The temple, in this case the temple in the Northern Kingdom, for it is to Israel that this is addressed, would have been the place where songs of joy were sung. Like the true Temple, it would have been designed as a place to rejoice in their gods. But once

God withdrew His presence and the Assyrians came into the land, the songs of the temple would turn to howlings, wailings, broken-hearted sounds of anguish. But further, we read, *there shall be many dead bodies in every place; they shall cast them forth with silence.*

People would come to their temple, supposedly a place of singing, and would see dead bodies lying everywhere. They would begin to wail. And then, realizing that may attract deadly attention, they would choke back even those wails and just silently carry the dead bodies out of the "happy/holy place" and throw them out into the street or some gully out of sight.

The basket of fruit afforded to them by their wickedness and rebellion would be rotten and deadly.

A bitter fury

Amos 8:4 *Hear this, O ye that swallow up the needy, even to make the poor of the land to fail,*

God paints some very vivid word pictures. He has just gotten done telling them about a basket of fruit, a rotten and deadly basket of fruit. He moves right from there to reminding them that they *swallow up the needy*. Their basket of fruit was what they were reaping directly because of what they had sown; they swallowed up the needy; God would give them fruit that they could not swallow.

Their swallowing up of the needy was to such a degree that they would *make the poor of the land to fail*. And in these words, we find the beginning of yet another play on words. *Fail* is from the word *shabath*. It means to cease, to desist. You will find the same word in nearly identical form in the very next verse:

Amos 8:5 *Saying, When will the new moon be gone, that we may sell corn? and the **sabbath**, that we may set forth wheat,* *making the ephah small, and the shekel great, and falsifying the balances by deceit?*

Fail and Sabbath are those matching words. They both mean to bring something to a stop. On the Sabbath day, work was to be eliminated. In Israel, they were causing the poor to be eliminated.

A fairly remarkable thing occurs in verse five. Amos accurately records the words of the people who were saying, *When will the new moon be gone, that we may sell corn? and the sabbath...*

The people of the Northern Kingdom were still observing many of the religious formalities of the Southern Kingdom, including the Sabbath. They had rejected God in favor of their idols, or at best, merely chosen to include Him along with their idols, and yet they still went through the motions as if they were the people of God.

When referencing those religious festivals, though, we find one of the problems; a problem that Amos had, in fact, just mentioned. Just like we see when Judah returned from captivity in Babylon, though they observed the Sabbath, they hated it because it interfered with their profits. Look again at what they said here:

...When will the new moon [a day they regarded as holy, though not specified by Mosaic law] *be gone, that we may sell corn? and the* **sabbath**, *that we may set forth wheat, making the ephah small, and the shekel great, and falsifying the balances by deceit?*

They were observing the Sabbath but hated every minute of it because they were not allowed to buy and sell, or to cheat people. They could not break out their rigged scales and false measures and sucker people into paying for more than they were getting because that would be "violating the Sabbath."

Heaven forbid they should have to wait till the next day to cheat people in order to "please God;" the irony is utterly breathtaking.

But there was more that made them wish every Sabbath day was already past:

Amos 8:6 *That we may buy the poor for silver, and the needy for a pair of shoes; yea, and sell the refuse of the wheat?*

God mentioned this same accusation against them early in chapter two. Rather than redeeming and relieving their poor countrymen, they were buying them up as bargains with their silver and then selling the needy so they could have a good pair of shoes with the profit they made from the transaction.

They were also selling *the refuse of the wheat.* They were selling poor-quality, useless wheat as if it were a good product, knowing that the poor people who would be buying it did not have the money or the means to fight back against them for what they were doing or any means to come up with other food on their own.

God would not take kindly to any of that:

Amos 8:7 *The LORD hath sworn by the excellency of Jacob, Surely I will never forget any of their works.*

From time to time, you will see commentators take this phrase, *the Lord has sworn by the excellency of Jacob*, as a reference to Himself as the excellency of Jacob. But in the context of the book of Amos, the exact opposite is true. Look back at what He said just a couple of chapters ago:

Amos 6:8 *The Lord GOD hath sworn by himself, saith the LORD the God of hosts, <u>I abhor the excellency of Jacob</u>, and hate his palaces: therefore will I deliver up the city with all that is therein.*

Clearly, God is not saying that He abhors Himself; therefore, He is not referring to Himself in Amos 8:7. The excellency of Jacob that He swore by in chapter eight and abhors in chapter six is the high and lofty position of prominence that He Himself brought them to. God is now swearing by the best that Israel has ever been under His hand that He will never forget these wicked things that they have done. In so many words, especially when you see Him add *therefore will I deliver up the city with all that is therein,* just as people often swear on their mama's graves, God is doing something more ominous: He is swearing on their graves.

Amos 8:8 *Shall not the land tremble for this* [for all they have done to the poor and all the judgment I am bringing because of that], *and every one mourn that dwelleth therein? and it shall rise up wholly as a flood; and it shall be cast out and drowned, as by the flood of Egypt.*

In these words, God is speaking of the land and painting a picture of it rising in the waters of the flood and being cast out and drowned, just as the flood waters of the Nile River pick up massive quantities of land and move it every time it overflows its banks. This was nothing less than the destruction of the land by Assyria being spoken of, something that God will, in the very next verse, paint yet another dramatic picture of.

Amos 8:9 *And it shall come to pass in that day, saith the Lord GOD, that I will cause the sun to go down at noon, and I will darken the earth in the clear day:*

In that day, the day spoken of in verse eight, when Assyria floods the land with people and carries so many of them away, God said that He would *cause the sun to go down at noon, and I will darken the earth in the clear day.* This is a word picture that He used frequently throughout the writings of the prophets:

Isaiah 59:10 *We grope for the wall like the blind, and we grope as if we had no eyes: <u>we stumble at noonday as in the night</u>; we are in desolate places as dead men.*

Jeremiah 15:9 *She that hath borne seven languisheth: she hath given up the ghost;* her sun is gone down while it was yet day: *she hath been ashamed and confounded: and the residue of them will I deliver to the sword before their enemies, saith the LORD.*

Micah 3:6 *Therefore night shall be unto you, that ye shall not have a vision; and it shall be dark unto you, that ye shall not divine; and* the sun shall go down over the prophets, and the day shall be dark over them.

This is still very common terminology in our day. We often speak of the sun setting on someone's life or ministry, or even of the sun setting on a nation or empire. It is a picture of the death of something that once seemed as if it would last forever.

Amos 8:10 *And I will turn your feasts into mourning, and all your songs into lamentation; and I will bring up sackcloth upon all loins, and baldness upon every head; and I will make it as the mourning of an only son, and the end thereof as a bitter day.*

This is the second time in this chapter that God has spoken of turning their feasts into mourning and their songs into lamentations; He did so in verse three with the words *the songs of the temple shall be howlings in that day*. Here, though, He adds that He will *bring up sackcloth upon all loins, and baldness upon every head; and I will make it as the mourning of an only son, and the end thereof as a bitter day.*

Sackcloth was the rough, scratchy fabric used for things like sacks of grain. For a person to be wearing something like that indicated great disaster and devastation.

The next thing God mentioned was that He would bring baldness upon every head. This was also a sign of great brokenness. Here is, perhaps, the most famous example of that in Scripture:

Job 1:20 *Then Job arose, and rent his mantle, and shaved his head, and fell down upon the ground, and worshipped,*

When Job lost it all, he shaved his head as an outward sign of how devastated and broken he was.

God had Amos end the verse with the words *I will make it* [that day of judgment] *as the mourning of an only son, and the end thereof as a bitter day.*

Israel's destruction would be as heartbreaking as a parent who had to endure the death of their only son; no day could end in any more of a bitter way.

Israel truly was facing a bitter fury.

A breathtaking famine

Amos 8:11 *Behold, the days come, saith the Lord GOD, that I will send a famine in the land, not a famine of bread, nor a thirst for water, but of hearing the words of the LORD:*

I rather suspect that anyone listening as Amos uttered these words to the people was at first terrified and then utterly confused. When God promised to send a famine, it normally meant a whole lot of people were going to starve to death; a truly horrible way to go. But in this case, after proclaiming that God was going to send a famine, he quickly specified that it would not be a famine of food or water but of the Word.

Up to this point in Scripture, prophets had uttered the words *Thus saith the LORD* 389 times. God sent judges and priests and prophets and even kings to communicate the word of the LORD to the people. You can find very few times or instances throughout the Old Testament up until the days of Amos in which God was not somehow communicating His Word to Israel. God communicating with His people was such a commonplace occurrence that they grew to where they could just brush it off and ignore it and treat it as if it was nothing special when, in reality, it was the most special thing any nation had ever experienced.

All of that was going to change. God was going to remove the Word from them; Scripture, prophets, prophecies, God was going to take those blessings away and leave His people without divine guidance.

How would these people respond, this nation who had so often despised the Word of the LORD? Remember, Amaziah had just told Amos to run back to Judah and not prophesy the Word of the LORD there in Israel. So, how would they react when they finally got what they wanted? The next verse gives that answer.

Amos 8:12 *And they shall wander from sea to sea, and from the north even to the east, they shall run to and fro to seek the word of the LORD, and shall not find it.*

From sea to sea meant from the Mediterranean to the Dead Sea; that covered from the west to the south. He then mentions from the north to the east as well, without assigning any geographical locations to them. So, Israel would run to every point of the compass. People would scatter out throughout the entirety of the land, trying to find a prophet or a piece of Scripture, some guidance from God to tell them how to handle the problems they were having, and there would be none to be found.

What they would not listen to when they could, they then could not listen to when they would.

Amos 8:13 *In that day shall the fair virgins and young men faint for thirst.*

The thirst of verse thirteen goes back to the thirst of verse eleven; this is still a thirst for the Word of the LORD that is being spoken of. When the calamity finally came, having pushed God and His word away for so very long, it would be the young people who bore the brunt of the disaster. They would run around seeking the Word of the LORD that their parents and their elders had pushed away for so long, and they would not be able to find it. It would do the older people well in every country, clime, and circumstance to remember that the results of the poor decisions we make will land most heavily on our children and grandchildren after us.

Amos 8:14 *They that swear by the sin of Samaria, and say, Thy god, O Dan, liveth; and, The manner of Beersheba liveth; even they shall fall, and never rise up again.*

Amos closes this chapter with three references to the idolatry of the people. The first one is the sin of Samaria.

This is the only place in the Bible where the phrase *the sin of Samaria is found*. It is a reference to the idol found in Bethel, just outside of Samaria. (Henry, 1264)

The second reference is found in the words *Thy god, O Dan, liveth*. This referred to one of Jeroboam's golden calves that was housed there in Dan. And the irony is, they were looking at this dead, non-moving, non-breathing, non-seeing, non-hearing thing made by people and with utter adoration saying, "It's alive!"

No, it really wasn't.

The third reference is found in the words *The manner of Beersheba liveth*. Manner is from the word *derek*, and it indicates a way of life. They were saying, "Your religion is alive and well, Beersheba!"

But it wasn't. It was the dead worship of a dead thing in defiance of the living God.

Here was God's judgment on Israel because of all of that idolatrous adoration: *they shall fall, and never rise up again*. And they did. They never thought they would, but they did. That ten-tribe kingdom of Israel was wiped out and ceased to exist. People from those ten tribes trickled back into the land through the years, but that kingdom ceased to exist when Assyria ran roughshod over them.

Fruit has a shelf life. And when that fruit is a nation that has turned its back on God, that shelf life can be very short indeed. It was in Israel's case. And the famine that followed was both unthinkable and unnecessary. All they ever had to do was listen to the Word of the LORD and obey the Word of the LORD, and they would never have been without the Word of the LORD.

This isn't just true of Israel—or of nations—it is true of each and every one of us, even now.

Chapter Fourteen
The Most Unlikely "Happily Ever After"

Amos 9:1 *I saw the Lord standing upon the altar: and he said, Smite the lintel of the door, that the posts may shake: and cut them in the head, all of them; and I will slay the last of them with the sword: he that fleeth of them shall not flee away, and he that escapeth of them shall not be delivered.* **2** *Though they dig into hell, thence shall mine hand take them; though they climb up to heaven, thence will I bring them down:* **3** *And though they hide themselves in the top of Carmel, I will search and take them out thence; and though they be hid from my sight in the bottom of the sea, thence will I command the serpent, and he shall bite them:* **4** *And though they go into captivity before their enemies, thence will I command the sword, and it shall slay them: and I will set mine eyes upon them for evil, and not for good.* **5** *And the Lord GOD of hosts is he that toucheth the land, and it shall melt, and all that dwell therein shall mourn: and it shall rise up wholly like a flood; and shall be drowned, as by the flood of Egypt.* **6** *It is he that buildeth his stories in the heaven, and hath founded his troop in the earth; he that calleth for the waters of the sea, and poureth them out upon the face of the earth: The LORD is his name.* **7** *Are ye not as children of the Ethiopians unto me, O children of Israel? saith the LORD. Have not I brought up Israel out of the land of Egypt? and the Philistines from Caphtor, and the Syrians from Kir?* **8** *Behold,* the eyes of the Lord GOD are upon the sinful kingdom, and I will destroy it from off the face of the earth; saving that I will not utterly destroy the house of Jacob, saith the LORD. **9** *For, lo, I will command, and I will sift the house of Israel among all nations, like as corn is sifted in a sieve, yet shall not the least grain fall upon the earth.* **10** *All the sinners of my people shall die by the sword, which say, The evil shall not overtake nor prevent us.* **11** *In that day will I raise up the tabernacle of David that is fallen, and close up the breaches thereof; and I will raise up his ruins, and I will build it as in the days of old:* **12** *That they may possess the remnant of Edom, and of all the heathen, which are called by my name, saith the LORD that doeth this.* **13** *Behold, the days come, saith the LORD, that the plowman shall overtake the reaper, and the treader of grapes him that soweth seed; and the mountains shall drop sweet wine, and all the hills shall melt.* **14** *And I will bring again the captivity of my people of Israel, and they shall build the waste cities, and inhabit them; and they shall plant vineyards, and drink the wine thereof; they shall also make gardens, and eat the fruit of them.* **15** *And I will plant them upon their land, and they shall no more be pulled up out of their land which I have given them, saith the LORD thy God.*

God sent word down to Tekoa to a hillbilly named Amos, a word that Amos was to go and prophesy in the Northern Kingdom. The message that He gave him was not a positive one; all throughout was judgment and woe. Along the way in delivering that prophecy, Amos was accosted by one of the false prophets there in Bethel, a charlatan named Amaziah. Amaziah told him to run back home to Judah and do his prophesying there because they did not want to hear it in Israel. But, true man of God that he was, Amos stood fast and refused to move or to cease. He not only continued his word against Israel, he also gave very personal words of judgment against Amaziah and his household. And then he went right back in the previous chapter and continued showing the visions and the judgments of God, specifically a basket of summer fruit that would then lead to a famine of the Word.

Now, as we enter this, the final chapter of the book of Amos, we will find it beginning the same way it has commenced throughout: judgment, woe, and ruin.

But it will not end that way.

A smiting

Amos 9:1 *I saw the Lord standing upon the altar: and he said, Smite the lintel of the door, that the posts may shake: and cut them in the head, all of them; and I will slay the last of them with the sword: he that fleeth of them shall not flee away, and he that escapeth of them shall not be delivered.*

Perhaps the best way to describe how Amos 9 begins is with the word "abrupt." With no lead-in, Amos simply says, *I saw the Lord standing upon the altar*.

Lord is not in all caps. This is the word for "*Adonay*", and it generally indicates *Lord* in a bit of a personal sense, something like "my Lord." Amos saw something others could not see; God peeled back the veil of the unseen world for him, and he saw God, his Lord, standing on the altar.

Amos was prophesying in the Northern Kingdom, Israel. He was right then in Bethel, the place that Amaziah called "the king's chapel and the king's court" in Amos 7:13. So the altar was not the real altar to the real God down south in Jerusalem; the altar God was standing on was the idolatrous altar of the golden calf of Jeroboam.

Let that one sink in; God stepped on one of the devil's altars.

Amos did not just see God standing; He also heard God speaking:

...and he said, Smite the lintel of the door, that the posts may shake: and cut them in the head, all of them; and I will slay the last of them with the sword: he that fleeth of them shall not flee away, and he that escapeth of them shall not be delivered.

The lintel of the door was the beam that went across the top, joining the wall on one side of the door to the wall on the other side of the door and providing support for anything resting on it above the door. By smiting that, the posts of the temple would indeed shake; this was damaging a critical part of the structure.

The *them* that God commanded to cut in the head were the idolatrous priests and worshippers who were going to scatter and run when the temple started crumbling around them. God was so angry with the whole lot of them by that point that He determined to allow none to survive; He said, *and I will slay the last of them with the sword: he that fleeth of them shall not flee away, and he that escapeth of them shall not be delivered.*

This matter of idolatry was clearly not going to end well for Israel.

A seeking

The story of the next few verses is going to center around five *thoughs* from God, none of which were positive. Verse two gives us the first couple of them.

Amos 9:2 Though *they dig into hell, thence shall mine hand take them;* **though** *they climb up to heaven, thence will I bring them down:*

He is still talking about the people from verse one who would go running, trying to escape the destruction God would bring down on them by means of the Assyrians. The word picture He used was designed to be both fantastical and stark.

Could they really dig into Hell? No. But if they somehow could, God would still reach down into those fiery depths and take them for judgment. Could they really climb up to Heaven? No. But if they somehow could, God would pluck them right off the street of gold and bring them back down for the purpose of judgment.

Verse three gives us the next *though:*

Amos 9:3 *And* ***though*** *they hide themselves in the top of Carmel, I will search and take them out thence;*

Hiding themselves in the top of Carmel may sound out of place; it seems like it was the only thing, thus far, they perhaps could have actually done. Mount Carmel was only sixty-two miles from Bethel, and the top of Carmel is a doable 1,791 feet above sea level. It has a tremendous number of caves that people throughout the long centuries fled to when they needed somewhere to hide. In reality, though, it was, for all practical purposes, just about as impossible as all of the rest. That sixty-two-mile trip, followed by a 1,791-foot climb, would have to be done by wading through the entire Assyrian army to get there.

Even if they could somehow make it the sixty-two miles past all of the Assyrian soldiers, and even if they could make that climb, God said that He would *search and take them out thence* for the purposes of judgment.

The next *though* is found at the end of verse three: *and* ***though*** *they be hid from my sight in the bottom of the sea, thence will I command the serpent, and he shall bite them:*

Could they actually hide in the bottom of the sea? No. But even if they somehow could, God would command a serpent to go there and bite them.

This reference, by the way, is an incredibly interesting one. For a very long time, sea serpents were regarded as nothing more than mythology. The first secular documentation of a sea serpent was in the relatively modern day, A.D. 1639. But nearly two thousand years before that, God was talking to Amos about them and saying that He would use them in judgment if needed.

And it was not an idle threat. The *Times Of India* put out a very recent column headlined "7 Venomous Sea Snakes That Are More Deadly Than The King Cobra."

Here is an excerpt:

> "The sea conceals some of the planet's most deadly inhabitants, and among them are the planet's most venomous sea snakes. These deadly snakes, unlike their land-dwelling relatives, slither through the ocean with ease, carrying venom so deadly that it can kill a human in a matter of hours. The silent killers reside in tropical seas from the Indian Ocean to the Pacific, going undetected—until too late. Others are so poisonous that they can kill thousands with only a few milligrams of venom." (7 venomous sea snakes)

The final *though* is in verse four:

Amos 9:4 *And **though** they go into captivity before their enemies, thence will I command the sword, and it shall slay them: and I will set mine eyes upon them for evil, and not for good.*

Many of those who survived the onslaught and invasion would be taken into captivity; a great many would likely surrender for that very purpose rather than be slaughtered. And that may well have had them thinking that, at the very least, they were, in fact, going to survive. But God was so angry by this point that He was even going to come after them in their captivity to slay them. They were going to have His full attention in the worst kind of way; He said, *and I will set mine eyes upon them for evil, and not for good*. Every moment that He looked at them, which would just so happen to be every moment, it would be to visit evil on them rather than good.

Amos 9:5 *And the Lord GOD of hosts is he that toucheth the land, and it shall melt, and all that dwell therein shall mourn: and it shall rise up wholly like a flood; and shall be drowned, as by the flood of Egypt.*

A word in verse five paints a fairly vivid picture for us. Amos said, *the Lord GOD of hosts is he that **toucheth** the land.* Toucheth is from the word *nahga*. Let me show you another place it is used in Scripture that really demonstrates what it means:

Exodus 19:12 *And thou shalt set bounds unto the people round about, saying, Take heed to yourselves, that ye go not up into the mount, or **touch** the border of it: whosoever **toucheth** the mount shall be surely put to death:* **13** *There shall not an hand **touch** it, but he shall surely be stoned, or shot through; whether it be beast or man, it shall not live: when the trumpet soundeth long, they shall come up to the mount.*

All three of those are from that same word, *nahga*. The vast majority of the time it is used, it indicates the exact same thing we see here, merely reaching out and touching something. God did not say that He was going to pick them up and shake them, or pound them into the ground, or throttle them; He simply said that He was going to *touch* the land, with the result being that the land would melt under the judgment.

What they would see with their eyes would be the Assyrians setting fires left and right, burning and melting everything in sight. What they would not see with their eyes was the God who was reaching out and touching the land to make it all happen.

God said of this: *and all that dwell therein shall mourn: and it shall rise up wholly like a flood; and shall be drowned, as by the flood of Egypt.* This goes right back to the picture of Amos 8:8, which used nearly identical words.

Amos 9:6 *It is he that buildeth his stories in the heaven, and hath founded his troop in the earth; he that calleth for the waters of the sea, and poureth them out upon the face of the earth: The LORD is his name.*

Amos is continuing his description of the God who will be bringing all of this judgment. In order for Him to do all that He has threatened, He must be of limitless power. And He is. Amos said, *It is he that buildeth his stories in the heaven, and hath founded his troop in the earth*. We still speak in our day of stories in a building. But we did not invent multi-story structures; people in Bible days were well familiar with the concept:

Genesis 6:16 *A window shalt thou make to the ark, and in a cubit shalt thou finish it above; and the door of the ark shalt thou set in the side thereof; with lower, second, and third* **stories** *shalt thou make it.*

Ezekiel 42:4 *And before the chambers was a walk of ten cubits breadth inward, a way of one cubit; and their doors toward the north. 5 Now the upper chambers were shorter: for the galleries were higher than these, than the lower, and than the middlemost of the building. 6 For they were in* **three stories**, *but had not pillars as the pillars of the courts: therefore the building was straitened more than the lowest and the middlemost from the ground.*

Heaven is not a single-layered structure; in fact, since God is the builder, it is pretty safe to say that there are more stories to it than any manmade structure could ever conceive of. And the God who did it would be the One bringing the judgment on Israel.

But Amos also described Him as the One who *hath founded his troop in the earth*. In this instance in Scripture, *troop* is from the word *agudah*. The other place in the Bible where *agudah* is rendered as troop is 2 Samuel 2:25:

2 Samuel 2:25 *And the children of Benjamin gathered themselves together after Abner, and became one **troop**, and stood on the top of an hill.*

So, what is God's troop in Amos 9:6? The last half of that verse answers the question for us:

...he that calleth for the waters of the sea, and poureth them out upon the face of the earth: The LORD is his name.

The same God whose name is the LORD, Jehovah, Who had and has enough power to make a multi-layered Heaven, also had and has enough power to use the waters of the sea on Earth as His personal troops to bring judgment on disobedient man. With a simple thought, God could cause a tsunami or other cataclysmic event to flood this entire world and destroy all of mankind.

Amos 9:7 *Are ye not as children of the Ethiopians unto me, O children of Israel? saith the LORD. Have not I brought up Israel out of the land of Egypt? and the Philistines from Caphtor, and the Syrians from Kir?*

One thing you must understand about Israel is that they, with every fiber of their being, believed that they were the most special people on Earth because God chose them above others. And they took that to the level of believing that God would never cast them off, no matter what. So, to hear God through Amos say, *Are ye not as children of the Ethiopians unto me, O children of Israel?* was an unfathomable shock to them.

The Ethiopians, descended from Cush, a son of Ham, were despised and looked down upon as heathens. And this was such a universal thought of the Jews that they even dared come against Moses over his marriage to an Ethiopian woman:

Numbers 12:1 *And Miriam and Aaron spake against Moses because of the Ethiopian woman whom he had married: for he had married an Ethiopian woman.*

This was a really big deal to them! For God to tell them that He now looked at them like they had always looked at the Ethiopians was like a knife to the heart. There was a second part to why they believed they were so special, though, namely that God brought them up out of Egypt into their land. With that in mind, look at the last half of verse seven again:

...Have not I brought up Israel out of the land of Egypt? and the Philistines from Caphtor, and the Syrians from Kir?

When God said, *Have not I brought up Israel out of the land of Egypt?* their reaction would have been an excited, proud, "Yes! Yes, you did! You brought us out of Egypt and into our Promised Land. We are special!" Unfortunately for them, He did not stop there. He did not even pause there. He went immediately into the words *and the Philistines from Caphtor, and the Syrians from Kir?* The thought runs something like this. "Hey Israel, I brought you from where you were to where you are—just exactly like I brought those you loathe and despise, the Philistines and Syrians, from where they were to where they are."

If "ouch" could be measured in tonnage, that bit of it would take a few dump truck loads to haul.

But God still was not done:

Amos 9:8 *Behold, the eyes of the Lord GOD are upon the sinful kingdom, and I will destroy it from off the face of the earth; saving that I will not utterly destroy the house of Jacob, saith the LORD.*

This may well be one of the most essential overlooked verses in the Bible. In thirty-eight short words, God distinguishes between Israel the kingdom and Israel the people. He makes it very plain that He absolutely will bring an end to the Northern Kingdom, but He absolutely will not bring an end to the house of Jacob.

God's promises to Abraham stand sure to this day—and forever. The antisemites of the world can hate it just as much as they hate most of the rest of Scripture, but God is not done with the Jews, has not set the Jews aside, has not replaced the Jews with the church, and will fulfill every Old Testament promise that He made to them.

A sifting

Amos 9:9 *For, lo, I will command, and I will sift the house of Israel among all nations, like as corn is sifted in a sieve, yet shall not the least grain fall upon the earth.* **10** *All the sinners of my people shall die by the sword, which say, The evil shall not overtake nor prevent us.*

These verses describe a marvelous miracle and a meticulous methodology.

God said that He would command and sift the house of Israel among the nations like corn is sifted in a sieve. In the sifting process, the grains, corns of wheat as Jesus called them in John 12:24, would be put into a screen and shaken back and forth so that the dust and the chaff could fall away. In that process, in normal human hands, sometimes a tiny grain or two might be lost. And yet, God's promise here concerning His people, the descendants of Abraham, Isaac, and Jacob, was that the least grain, the smallest, and most insignificant among them, would not fall to the earth.

In verse ten, He said that all of the sinners of His people would die by the sword, *those which say the evil shall not overtake, nor prevent* [meet, go before] *us*. When you put all of that picture together, you see that the sinners of His people were the dust and the chaff, and the righteous among His people were the grains, some great and some small.

God would send the ten tribes into captivity and dispersion among all the nations; He would sift them in those places and in that method. But when all was said and done, it would only be the sinners of the house of Abraham, Isaac, and Jacob that would be lost forever. There would be a righteous remnant of all ten of those tribes brought back into the land.

When God sifts, He does it perfectly, and nothing that should be saved is ever lost.

A settling

All has seemed very bleak thus far in chapter nine. In fact, in the entire book of Amos, there has been scarcely so much as a single ray of hope. But since God just got done alluding to the future restoration of a righteous remnant, the book of Amos actually ends with hope—the most unlikely "Happily Ever After."

Amos 9:11 *In that day will I raise up the tabernacle of David that is fallen, and close up the breaches thereof; and I will raise up his ruins, and I will build it as in the days of old:* **12** *That they may possess the remnant of Edom, and of all the heathen, which are called by my name, saith the LORD that doeth this.*

In that day, the day mentioned in verse ten when God sifts His people yet makes sure that not a single grain falls to the earth, God said that He would *raise up the tabernacle of David that is fallen, and close up the breaches thereof; and I will raise up his ruins, and I will build it as in the days of old:*

These words and the words that follow are quoted in the New Testament—and by what was once the least likely of men to speak them, namely James, the formerly disbelieving half-brother of Jesus:

Acts 15:16 *After this I will return, and will build again the tabernacle of David, which is fallen down; and I will build again the ruins thereof, and I will set it up:* **17** *That the residue of men might seek after the Lord, and all the Gentiles, upon* *whom my name is called, saith the Lord, who doeth all these things.*

When James quoted them, it was in reference to the last part, the part about the Gentiles being brought into the household of faith. When Amos first gave them, he started with Israel's restoration and then mentioned the bringing in of the Gentiles. The start, Israel's restoration, was expressed in these words: *In that day will I raise up the tabernacle of David that is fallen, and close up the breaches thereof; and I will raise up his ruins, and I will build it as in the days of old:*

Let me assure you, the people who first heard these words did not appreciate them at all. You see, in their day, *the tabernacle of David*, which, as we see from the entire sentence that stretches over verses eleven and twelve, clearly refers to the nation of Israel itself, had not yet fallen and therefore did not need to be raised up.

Future generations, though, would absolutely appreciate those words because they either saw that fall or were born in dispersion after it happened. They experienced the breaches, the massive gaps made in the once seemingly impenetrable walls of their fortified cities, both in the north and the south.

But it was going to be rebuilt. God said, *I will raise up his ruins, and I will build it as in the days of old*. The people, the land, the cities, all were going to be restored as during the years of their glory. And while an argument can be made for a partial fulfillment of that during the days of Christ, the ultimate fulfillment is yet to come. It will be during the Millennial Reign that Israel possesses all of her land, and her people flourish within it. It will be during the Millennial Reign that they will be a true monarchy once more.

But even before that time, God was going to do something else very special, another thing that the Jews both in Amos's day and even in James's day did not like. He said, *That* *they may possess the remnant of Edom, and of all the heathen, <u>which are called by my name</u>, saith the LORD that doeth this.*

The reference to Edom was somewhat fulfilled in the years prior to the coming of Christ. Through the Old Testament, Edom was almost always a strong people and a strong enemy of Israel, even though they were related. By the time of Christ, Idumea had largely been subjugated and assimilated. John Hyrcanus conquered it and them in 126 B.C. and forced them to convert to Judaism.

But that, too, had a much further-reaching fulfillment. In the words *which are called by my name,* we find that God was referring not merely to the military conquest of the Edomites but to the entire bringing in of the Gentile world through the gospel of Christ. That is how James took it when the Gentiles began to be saved in the Book of Acts, and he was entirely correct.

That began in earnest in the very first generation of Christianity and has continued for 2,000 years now. If you, dear reader, are saved, then you today are a part of the fulfillment of this prophecy of Amos.

The closing words of verse twelve, *saith the LORD that doeth this,* James paraphrased as *saith the Lord, who doeth all these things.* The "these things" of Acts 15 were all that was being reported by Paul and Barnabas and Peter, all of these Gentiles getting saved. Amos said that it was a work of the LORD; James said that it was a work of the LORD. In both cases, this was an admonition of the Jews not to resist it but rather to embrace it.

After having alluded to that, though, Amos segued directly back into a discussion of Israel in the latter days:

Amos 9:13 *Behold, the days come, saith the LORD, that the plowman shall overtake the reaper, and the treader of grapes him that soweth seed; and the mountains shall drop sweet wine, and all the hills shall melt.*

The picture described here is utterly abnormal in agricultural terms. There should simply be no circumstance in which the reapers and the plowers are working in the same field at the same time on the same crop. And yet, God was promising that their fields and vineyards would produce such massive, miraculous amounts of produce that they were still trying to gather it all in when it came time to sow the field for the next season.

All of it, *the treader of grapes him that soweth seed; and the mountains shall drop sweet wine, and all the hills shall melt* [dissolved by the flow of sweet wine, rather than in judgment as in verse five], picture such a coming prosperity that all of the heartache Amos prophesied in the interim, and that has come to pass, would and will be forgotten.

Amos 9:14 *And I will bring again the captivity of my people of Israel, and they shall build the waste cities, and inhabit them; and they shall plant vineyards, and drink the wine thereof; they shall also make gardens, and eat the fruit of them.*

This promise of God through Amos is not an isolated one in Scripture. You really need to get a grasp of how often God made promises like this to truly understand how serious He was about eventually fully restoring Israel. Here is a sampling:

Isaiah 61:4 *And they shall build the old wastes, they shall raise up the former desolations, and they shall repair the waste cities, the desolations of many generations.*

Isaiah 65:21 *And they shall build houses, and inhabit them; and they shall plant vineyards, and eat the fruit of them.*

Jeremiah 30:3 *For, lo, the days come, saith the LORD, that I will bring again the captivity of my people Israel and Judah, saith the LORD: and I will cause them to return to the land that I gave to their fathers, and they shall possess it.*

Jeremiah 30:18 *Thus saith the LORD; Behold, I will bring again the captivity of Jacob's tents, and have mercy on his* *dwellingplaces; and the city shall be builded upon her own heap, and the palace shall remain after the manner thereof.*

Ezekiel 36:33 *Thus saith the Lord GOD; In the day that I shall have cleansed you from all your iniquities I will also cause you to dwell in the cities, and the wastes shall be builded.* **34** *And the desolate land shall be tilled, whereas it lay desolate in the sight of all that passed by.* **35** *And they shall say, This land that was desolate is become like the garden of Eden; and the waste and desolate and ruined cities are become fenced, and are inhabited.* **36** *Then the heathen that are left round about you shall know that I the LORD build the ruined places, and plant that that was desolate: I the LORD have spoken it, and I will do it.*

I could give you many more. God made this particular set of promises over and over and over again. He promised to bring Israel back from their captivity, reestablish them in their land, make them a true monarchy once again, and make them so prosperous that the entire world would envy them and the Gentiles would seek their favor. And <u>at absolutely no time since that day has all of this taken place!</u>

You really need to grasp this. Those who take the preterist view of Scripture, the idea that all of it has already been fulfilled (or at least such a huge percentage of it that it may as well be), are not paying the remotest bit of attention else they would never come to that conclusion. God still has a huge national plan for Israel, of which only their restoration to the land has been fulfilled in 1948.

That part, by the way, is irrevocable:

Amos 9:15 *And I will plant them upon their land, and* <u>*they shall no more be pulled up out of their land*</u> *which I have given them, saith the LORD thy God.*

Since Israel's rebirth as a nation in 1948, the Muslim/Arab nations around them have beat the drum for their destruction and extermination. All across college and university campuses here in the United States, leftists, illiterate of history and of Scripture, are chanting the deadly phrase "From the river to the sea, Palestine shall be free," which is nothing less than a call for the complete genocide of the Jewish people.

That satanic hatred will find its ultimate fulfillment during the Tribulation Period under the hand and rule of the Antichrist. But it will never succeed; God has planted His people in their land once more, and they will never be removed.

And yet, Amos spoke these concluding words as prophecy to people whom he had just scalded all the way to the bone and promised would be removed from their land for the time being. Their disobedience and idolatry caused God to decree the death of their kingdom and the dispersion of their people.

But in spite of it all, the God who loved them was going to restore them fully in the latter days.

How glorious that such a grim prophecy as that of Amos ends with such a glowing promise! This really was "The Most Unlikely Happily Ever After."

Obadiah
Turmoil In Edom

Chapter Fifteen
Have You Heard The Rumor About Edom?

Obadiah 1:1 *The vision of Obadiah. Thus saith the Lord GOD concerning Edom; We have heard a rumour from the LORD, and an ambassador is sent among the heathen, Arise ye, and let us rise up against her in battle.* **2** *Behold, I have made thee small among the heathen: thou art greatly despised.* **3** *The pride of thine heart hath deceived thee, thou that dwellest in the clefts of the rock, whose habitation is high; that saith in his heart, Who shall bring me down to the ground?* **4** *Though thou exalt thyself as the eagle, and though thou set thy nest among the stars, thence will I bring thee down, saith the LORD.* **5** *If thieves came to thee, if robbers by night, (how art thou cut off!) would they not have stolen till they had enough? if the grapegatherers came to thee, would they not leave some grapes?* **6** *How are the things of Esau searched out! how are his hidden things sought up!* **7** *All the men of thy confederacy have brought thee even to the border: the men that were at peace with thee have deceived thee, and prevailed against thee; they that eat thy bread have laid a wound under thee: there is none understanding in him.* **8** *Shall I not in that day, saith the LORD, even destroy the wise men out of Edom, and understanding out of the mount of Esau?* **9** *And thy mighty men, O Teman, shall be dismayed, to the end that every one of the mount of Esau may be cut off by slaughter.* **10** *For thy violence against thy brother Jacob shame shall cover thee, and thou shalt be cut off for ever.* **11** *In the day that thou stoodest on the other side, in the day that the strangers carried away captive his forces, and foreigners entered into his gates, and cast lots upon Jerusalem, even thou wast as one of them.* **12** *But thou shouldest not have looked on the day of thy brother in the day that he became a stranger;*

neither shouldest thou have rejoiced over the children of Judah in the day of their destruction; neither shouldest thou have spoken proudly in the day of distress. **13** *Thou shouldest not have entered into the gate of my people in the day of their calamity; yea, thou shouldest not have looked on their affliction in the day of their calamity, nor have laid hands on their substance in the day of their calamity;* **14** *Neither shouldest thou have stood in the crossway, to cut off those of his that did escape; neither shouldest thou have delivered up those of his that did remain in the day of distress.* **15** *For the day of the LORD is near upon all the heathen: as thou hast done, it shall be done unto thee: thy reward shall return upon thine own head.* **16** *For as ye have drunk upon my holy mountain, so shall all the heathen drink continually, yea, they shall drink, and they shall swallow down, and they shall be as though they had not been.* **17** *But upon mount Zion shall be deliverance, and there shall be holiness; and the house of Jacob shall possess their possessions.* **18** *And the house of Jacob shall be a fire, and the house of Joseph a flame, and the house of Esau for stubble, and they shall kindle in them, and devour them; and there shall not be any remaining of the house of Esau; for the LORD hath spoken it.* **19** *And they of the south shall possess the mount of Esau; and they of the plain the Philistines: and they shall possess the fields of Ephraim, and the fields of Samaria: and Benjamin shall possess Gilead.* **20** *And the captivity of this host of the children of Israel shall possess that of the Canaanites, even unto Zarephath; and the captivity of Jerusalem, which is in Sepharad, shall possess the cities of the south.* **21** *And saviours shall come up on mount Zion to judge the mount of Esau; and the kingdom shall be the LORD'S.*

Joel had written of turmoil in Judah. Amos had written of turmoil in Damascus, Gaza, Tyre, Edom, Ammon, Moab,

Judah, and Israel. In the book of Obadiah, just one chapter long, Edom will be the entire focus.

A mysterious prophet

Obadiah 1:1a *The vision of Obadiah.*

Even among the oft-enigmatic minor prophets, Obadiah is a mystery. Of this man, we know exactly one thing: his name, Obadiah, meaning *the servant of Jehovah*. Even that, though, is not much of a help to us; Obadiah was one of the more common names in the Old Testament, being borne by a fairly significant number of men.

With other prophets, we are usually given the names of their father: Hosea, the son of Beeri; Joel, the son of Pethuel; Jonah, the son of Amittai; Zephaniah, the son of Cushi; Zechariah, the son of Berechiah.

Sometimes, God instead gave us where or what people they were from: Amos, who was among the herdmen of Tekoa; Micah the Morasthite; Nahum the Elkoshite.

But with Obadiah, we are not given either of those. And unlike Hosea or Amos, nothing in the book that he wrote tells us anything about himself. Obadiah is, quite simply, the most mysterious of all of the minor prophets.

A marked target

Obadiah 1:1b *Thus saith the Lord GOD concerning Edom; We have heard a rumour from the LORD, and an ambassador is sent among the heathen, Arise ye, and let us rise up against her in battle.*

While Obadiah himself is a mystery, the target of his prophecy is anything but. God commissioned Obadiah to write exclusively against Edom, the people who were descended from Esau, the brother of Jacob. There was enmity between these two from their mother's womb, and the years that followed continued that pattern among the people that they produced. But from a practical standpoint, the enmity was one-sided; it was always strong Edom attacking Israel in her weakest moments. Israel was actually commanded by God to view this relationship the exact opposite way:

Deuteronomy 23:7a *Thou shalt not abhor an Edomite; for he is thy brother:*

That discrepancy, Israel not despising Edom but Edom despising Israel, is what this prophecy is all about. Thus, it is that we find the Lord GOD (adonay Jehovah) saying, *We have heard a rumour from the LORD, and an ambassador is sent among the heathen, Arise ye, and let us rise up against her in battle.*

These words are nearly identical to the words of Jeremiah, which seems to indicate that Obadiah was likely a late contemporary of Jeremiah, coming in on the end of Jeremiah's ministry and continuing on into the days of the Babylonian captivity:

Jeremiah 49:14 *I have heard a rumour from the LORD, and an ambassador is sent unto the heathen, saying, Gather ye together, and come against her, and rise up to the battle.*

With Jeremiah, it was: *I have heard a rumour from the LORD.* With Obadiah, it was: *We have heard a rumour from the LORD.* God is expanding the circle in Obadiah, obviously including another prophet other than Jeremiah, including Himself, and including everyone else to whom He sent this "rumor." Rumor is from the word *shemuah*, and it means tidings, news, a report. This rumor, then, this bit of news from God to man, was that *an ambassador is sent among the heathen,* and the ambassador's message was *Arise ye, and let us rise up against her* [Edom] *in battle.* God was going to use other heathen nations as His sword of judgment against Edom.

Obadiah 1:2 *Behold, I have made thee small among the heathen: thou art greatly despised.*

You should understand, at this point, that when Obadiah sent or spoke these words to Edom, they would have been scoffed at as ludicrous. Edom was, at the time of this prophecy, neither small among the heathen nor greatly despised by those heathen. Edom was a prosperous and powerful nation at that time, stretching from Dedan in Arabia all the way to Bozrah in the north (Jamieson, 2:565). In modern terms, that was from Northwest Saudi Arabia all the way to Jordan. That is nearly a thousand miles of territory.

Nonetheless, the judgment on them was so certain of a future occurrence that God phrased it in the present tense, saying, *I **have** made thee small among the heathen: thou **art** greatly despised.*

Obadiah 1:3 *The pride of thine heart hath deceived thee, thou that dwellest in the clefts of the rock, whose habitation is high; that saith in his heart, Who shall bring me down to the ground?*

We are now made privy to another thing that contributed to the pride and arrogance of Edom, which deceived their own hearts. They dwelt in the clefts of the rock; their habitation was high; they looked around and said in their hearts, *Who shall bring me down to the ground?*

The cities of Edom, and among them Petra, the capital, in the Wady Musa, were on high mountains and cut into the rocks. Petra is entirely shielded by rocks. The most noticeable thing about the mountains of Edom is the massive red sandstone rocks from which they were hewn. In the heart of those rocks, invisible from prying outside eyes, lay Petra, the then capital of Edom. (Jamieson, 2:565)

But God had a word to those arrogant Edomites who thought that their high rock cities could not be reached by God Himself:

Obadiah 1:4 *Though thou exalt thyself as the eagle, and though thou set thy nest among the stars, thence will I bring thee down, saith the LORD.*

God, in this verse, acknowledged their high position. It was as if they were eagles, safely set in a nest on the highest of the mountains, mountains so high that, for all practical purposes, they may as well have been among the stars themselves. But their high position did not daunt Him in the least; He said, *thence will I bring thee down, saith the LORD.* This was an answer to their challenging question in verse three: *Who shall bring me down to the ground?* God heard that and answered, "I will."

There is no perch so high that the hand of God cannot reach.

Obadiah 1:5 *If thieves came to thee, if robbers by night, (how art thou cut off!) would they not have stolen till they had enough? if the grapegatherers came to thee, would they not leave some grapes?*

There are two pictures and a parenthetical thought in this verse. Picture number one is that of a thief who would enter a house. No thief ever enters the house with the idea of stripping everything to the bare walls; they take what valuable things they can conveniently carry, and they leave. No grape gatherers ever gather every single tiny little grape off the vine; some will invariably be left behind.

Edom was not going to be given that consideration. In the parenthetical phrase *how art thou cut off!*, God was promising that the heathens He would send against them would take absolutely everything from them.

Something (which we will shortly see) had really gotten God angry with Edom.

Obadiah 1:6 *How are the things of Esau searched out! how are his hidden things sought up!*

God is still speaking of a future judgment in terms so certain that He phrases it as if it were a present, already completed reality. Verse six is tied to the thought of verse five. All of the things that Edom would have hidden in their house or vineyard, a picture of the nation itself, were going to be searched out and taken. Edom would be left bare and desolate by the time the heathens were done performing their task as the sword of God's judgment against them.

Obadiah 1:7 *All the men of thy confederacy have brought thee even to the border: the men that were at peace with thee have deceived thee, and prevailed against thee; they that eat thy bread have laid a wound under thee: there is none understanding in him.*

Like most nations throughout history, Edom formed alliances, confederacies, with other nations. Prominently among them, they formed an alliance with the Chaldeans (Babylonians) against Israel. And it would be those very Chaldeans whom they trusted to help them destroy their hated relatives that would eventually turn and destroy them as well.

The picture God painted here is very informative. He said *All the men of thy confederacy* [your allies] *have brought thee even to the border: the men that were at peace with thee have deceived thee, and prevailed against thee; they that eat thy bread have laid a wound under thee: there is none understanding in him.*

He is describing the day that Edom's allies, those that she trusted for help, would drive her to the borders of her own land so that she could be taken into captivity, and they could spoil and rob all of her goods in peace. They would prevail *against her* rather than for her. They ate her bread in peace at the table where they promised to ally with her and defend her, and then they wounded her by betraying her.

For all of that, though, which should have been obvious, God said, *there is none understanding in him* [any wise man of Edom]. For all of their famed wisdom and cunning, and in spite of the fact that God here clearly prophesied it, Edom would never see this coming.

Here is a bit about those wise men that I just mentioned:

Obadiah 1:8 *Shall I not in that day, saith the LORD, even destroy the wise men out of Edom, and understanding out of the mount of Esau?* **9** *And thy mighty men, O Teman* [one of the strongest parts of Edom], *shall be dismayed, to the end that every one of the mount of Esau may be cut off by slaughter.*

The wisdom of Edom was famed far and wide. Obadiah was not the only prophet to speak of it:

Jeremiah 49:7 *Concerning Edom, thus saith the LORD of hosts; Is wisdom no more in Teman? is counsel perished from the prudent? is their wisdom vanished?*

God was going to rob Edom of their wise men, or rob their wise men of their wisdom, for the purpose of seeing Edom destroyed. The Family Bible Notes makes a prescient note of this, saying, "When God purposes to destroy a nation for its sins, he commonly removes from it the wise and prudent, and gives it over to weak and foolish counsels." (Linder, Family Bible Notes)

If you do not see how frightening that is, simply listen to the average member of Congress speak on any given day of the week, and you will.

A malicious behavior

Obadiah 1:10 *For thy violence against thy brother Jacob shame shall cover thee, and thou shalt be cut off for ever.*

We now arrive at the crux of the matter, the reason that God was so furiously angry with Edom. All of this was because of their violence against their brother, Jacob, the nation of Israel. God was going to cover their glory with shame and cut them off forever because of how they treated His people, their own relatives.

If you are trying to think through Scripture for one particular instance of this, then you are missing the point entirely. It is not that Edom made one bad choice or even two or three bad choices to hate and come against Israel. It is that they did seemingly nothing but that at any time against Israel. Here is how Ezekiel the prophet put it concerning Edom:

Ezekiel 35:5 *Because thou hast had <u>a perpetual hatred</u>, and hast shed the blood of the children of Israel by the force of the sword in the time of their calamity, in the time that their iniquity had an end:*

It was perpetual. It was always. It was forever. Edom never *didn't* hate and try to ruin Israel. Seeing this, God finally had enough and determined to cut Edom off forever.

Obadiah 1:11 *In the day that thou stoodest on the other side, in the day that the strangers carried away captive his forces, and foreigners entered into his gates, and cast lots upon Jerusalem, even thou wast as one of them.*

This verse and the verses that follow are the reason that I earlier said that Obadiah probably continued on past the days of Jeremiah and on into the Babylonian captivity. What God describes here is the fall of Jerusalem to Babylon. And Edom's role in that is written about in Psalm 137:

Psalm 137:7 *Remember, O LORD, the children of Edom in the day of Jerusalem; who said, Rase it, rase it, even to the foundation thereof.*

To *rase* something is to strip it down and empty it. When Babylon came against their kinfolk, Judah, Edom stood there and cheered for Babylon against Judah, encouraging them to absolutely devastate her. They became *as one of them*, one of the Babylonians. They watched as those Babylonians cast lots, gambling to see who got to take which Jews for slaves and what spoil for their own, and they reveled in it all.

This was their own flesh and blood family whose destruction they were cheering. But more than that, this was God's chosen people, and He was not going to take what Edom did lightly or ever let it go.

Obadiah 1:12 *But thou shouldest not have looked on the day of thy brother in the day that he became a stranger; neither shouldest thou have rejoiced over the children of Judah in the day of their destruction; neither shouldest thou have spoken proudly in the day of distress.*

This was not a look of concern and anguish that God was so angry with; this was Edom looking on with pleasure and satisfaction as Judah was removed from their land and became strangers in another land. (Keil, 1:361)

They rejoiced at the day of Judah's destruction and spoke proudly in the day of Judah's distress. God was bitterly angry over both of those things and was not going to let it go.

But that does not yet exhaust the extent of why God was angry. The next two verses make up one long sentence that gives us an even more jaw-dropping reason for that fury:

Obadiah 1:13 *Thou shouldest not have entered into the gate of my people in the day of their calamity; yea, thou shouldest not have looked on their affliction in the day of their calamity, nor have laid hands on their substance in the day of their calamity;* **14** *Neither shouldest thou have stood in the crossway, to cut off those of his that did escape; neither shouldest thou have delivered up those of his that did remain in the day of distress.*

Edom did not just sit back and watch as the Babylonians conquered and ravaged Jerusalem; Edom came through the gates after them to grab what they could grab, like jackals coming in after the lions have made their kill. Worse, people from Edom, who knew the lay of the land far better than the Babylonians, stood around the city in the gaps and potential pathways of escape and turned back every Jew that they saw using those paths of escape. They also *delivered up those of his that did remain in the day of distress*, meaning they went and found those who were successfully hiding and turned them over to the enemy.

In all the ranks of sordid human history, there has rarely, if ever, been such an example of such depths of low-down sorriness as all of this.

A menacing pronouncement

Obadiah 1:15 *For the day of the LORD is near upon all the heathen: as thou hast done, it shall be done unto thee: thy reward shall return upon thine own head.*

We saw the day of the LORD five times in Joel, three times in Amos, and now we find it appearing in the singular chapter of Obadiah.

This day is a day of judgment. And in these words that Obadiah speaks to Edom, he both expands it to the final judgment of all the heathen nations and applies it specifically to Edom in his day as well. Edom was going to experience the law of sowing and reaping: as he had done to others, so it would be done to him. Judah, his brother, should have been able to count on him for assistance but was instead betrayed. Edom would likewise be betrayed by those whom he should have been able to trust.

Obadiah 1:16 *For as ye have drunk upon my holy mountain, so shall all the heathen drink continually, yea, they* *shall drink, and they shall swallow down, and they shall be as though they had not been.*

It is not Judah that is mentioned as drinking on God's holy mountain, as many commentators, for some reason, say. This is still Edom being spoken to and about. (Keil, 1:366). During their forays up to Jerusalem to watch the Babylonians destroy their kinsman, the Edomites had turned all of that into a festive party, drinking and enjoying with glee what they were watching. But the law of sowing and reaping that God espoused in the previous verse would apply here as well; in short, others would one day drink over their demise, and then they too would have their turn at judgment and disappear as if they had never existed.

God's people, though, despite their seeming helplessness and hopelessness, would ultimately fare far better:

Obadiah 1:17 *But upon mount Zion shall be deliverance, and there shall be holiness; and the house of Jacob shall possess their possessions.*

Obadiah and Jeremiah and most of the prophets spoke of Judah and Jerusalem in terms of ruin at the hands of the Babylonians. And yet, they also all spoke of them in terms of restoration, as Obadiah does here. God would and has delivered His people; seventy years was the captivity, and not a day longer. God can and will bring them to holiness:

Romans 11:26 *And so all Israel shall be saved: as it is written, There shall come out of Sion the Deliverer, and shall turn away ungodliness from Jacob:*

God can and will ensure that *the house of Jacob shall possess their possessions.* They will have all of their land, all of their treasures, all of the good things that God has promised them.

They would also have righteous retribution:

Obadiah 1:18 *And the house of Jacob shall be a fire, and the house of Joseph a flame, and the house of Esau for stubble, and they shall kindle in them, and devour them; and there shall not be any remaining of the house of Esau; for the LORD hath spoken it.*

This has already come to be. After their return from captivity, the Jews came against Edom, reduced them to slavery, and forced them to be circumcised and proselyte to Judaism. There may well be people genetically descended from Esau still alive somewhere on Earth, but there are no more Edomites; they were destroyed through assimilation. (Clarke, 4:696)

Obadiah 1:19 *And they of the south shall possess the mount of Esau; and they of the plain the Philistines: and they shall possess the fields of Ephraim, and the fields of Samaria: and Benjamin shall possess Gilead.*

This all happened, just as God said it would. After their return from captivity, the Jews who possessed the southern part of the land took possession of the mountains of Idumea which were contiguous to them. Those who lived in the plains took over the former territory of the Philistines.

The fields of Ephraim and Samaria were given to the Jews by Alexander the Great and later recaptured for the Jews by John Hyrcanus.

Benjamin went on to possess Gilead to the east. Edom and everyone else who was cheering the Jews demise went on to lose everything to the Jews. (Clarke, 4:696)

Obadiah 1:20 *And the captivity of this host of the children of Israel shall possess that of the Canaanites, even unto Zarephath; and the captivity of Jerusalem, which is in Sepharad, shall possess the cities of the south.*

As we arrive in the last two verses of the book of Obadiah, take a step back and expand your view, because that is exactly what God has Obadiah do. You see, while the other territories mentioned in previous verses went on to be possessed by the Jews, Zarephath up to the northwest, Canaanite territory, has not yet belonged to them. That is still to come during the Millennial Reign, if not before.

Lastly, there is the promise that *the captivity of Jerusalem, which is in Sepharad, shall possess the cities of the south.*

There is no place such as Sepharad known to history or archaeology. The name, though, means separated, or separation. This, then, is almost certainly a reference to the Jews of the diaspora, the dispersed Jews scattered throughout all the world during their times of exile. They will possess the unspecified *cities of the south.*

Obadiah 1:21 *And saviours* [yasha, deliverers] *shall come up on mount Zion to judge the mount of Esau; and the kingdom shall be the LORD'S.*

These saviors do not refer to the Savior; these are military deliverers, people from the time of the Maccabees all the way through the time when Christ the King comes again, people who have and will deliver their people from oppression and judge the mount of Esau, which in the larger sense here refers to all the heathens that ever come against them. The end of all this will be that the kingdom shall be the LORD's. Jehovah will come and establish the Millennial Kingdom after all of these long generations of trials and tribulations for the Jews and finally give them their full possession that they have waited for, for so very long.

That is good news for Israel.

It was not and never will be good news for their enemies.

Works Cited

7 venomous sea snakes in the world that are more deadly than the king cobra. The Times of India. (n.d.). https://timesofindia.indiatimes.com/etimes/trending/7-venomous-sea-snakes-in-the-world-that-are-more-deadly-than-king-cobra/amp_articleshow/118472096.cms (Accessed April 29, 2025)

Clarke, Adam. *The Holy Bible, Containing the Old and New Testaments, the Text Carefully Printed from the Most Correct Copies of the Present Authorized Translation, Including the Marginal Readings and Parallel Texts: with a Commentary and Critical Notes Designed as a Help to a Better Understanding of the Sacred Writings.* Vol. 6 Set, Abingdon, 1977.

Feinberg, C. L. (1976). *The minor prophets.* Moody Press.

Henry, M. (1935a). *Matthew Henry's Commentary on the Whole Bible* (Vol. 4). Fleming H. Revell Co.

Jamieson, R., Fausset, A. R., & Brown, D. (1997). *A commentary on the old and new testaments* (Vol. 2). Hendrickson Publishers.

Keil, C. F., & Delitzsch, F. (1961). *Biblical Commentary on The Old Testament; The Twelve Minor Prophets* (Vol. 1). Eerdmans.

Linder, Phil. Power Bible CD v 5.9, 2010

Orr, J. (1955). *The International Standard Bible Encyclopaedia.* W.B. Eerdmans Pub. Co.

Roussi, A. (2020, March 12). *Why gigantic locust swarms are challenging governments and researchers.* Nature News. https://www.nature.com/articles/d41586-020-00725-x#:~:text=Swarms%20typically%20can%20occupy%20100,would%20eat%20in%20a%20day (Accessed January 9, 2025)

Other Books by Pastor Bo Wagner

Colossians: The Treasures of Deity
Daniel: Breathtaking
Ephesians: The Treasures of Family
Esther: Five Feasts and the Fingerprints of God
Galatians: Treasures of Liberty
Hosea: Love When It Matters Most
James: The Pen and the Plumb Line
Jonah: A Story of Greatness
Nehemiah: A Labor of Love
Philippians: The Treasures of Joy
Proverbs Vol 1: Bright Light from Dark Sayings
Proverbs Vol 2: Bright Light from Dark Sayings
The Revelation: Ready or Not
Romans: Salvation from A-Z
Ruth: Diamonds in the Darkness

Beyond the Colored Coat
From Footers to Finish Nails
Learning Not to Fear the Old Testament
Marriage Makers/Marriage Breakers
I'm Saved! Now What???
Don't Muzzle the Ox
Why Christmas?

Books in the Night Heroes Series

Cry from the Coal Mine (Vol 1)
Free Fall (Vol 2)
Broken Brotherhood (Vol 3)
The Blade of Black Crow (Vol 4)
Ghost Ship (Vol 5)

When Serpents Rise (Vol 6)
Moth Man (Vol 7)
Runaway (Vol 8)
Terror by Day (Vol 9)
Winter Wolf (Vol 10)
Desert Heat (Vol 11)
Deadline (Vol 12)
The Sword and the Iron Curtain (Vol 13)

Other Fiction

Zak Blue: Falcon Wing
Zak Blue: Enter the Maelstrom

Devotionals

DO Drops Vol. 1
DO Drops Vol. 2
DO Drops Vol. 3
DO Drops Vol. 4
DO Drops Vol. 5
DO Drops Vol. 6
DO Drops Vol. 7
DO Drops Vol. 8
DO Drops Vol. 9
DO Drops Vol 10
DO Drops Vol 11
DO Drops Vol 12
DO Drops Vol 13

www.ingramcontent.com/pod-product-compliance
Lightning Source LLC
LaVergne TN
LVHW051115080426
835510LV00018B/2047